Fundraising and Fundraising Ideas

The Complete Fundraising Bible

How to Maximize Your Profits From Your
Fundraising Events.

By

Vera Gregory

CW00801415

Table of Contents

Introduction

Money is fundamental to researching serious illnesses, fighting drug abuse and domestic violence, supplying urban schools with necessary computer equipment, sheltering the homeless, and helping those affected by violent crime and acts of terrorism. No matter what your cause, you will likely need to raise money at some point.

This book focuses not only on how the modern fundraiser goes about procuring money in a highly competitive world, but also on how he or she can best reach out and touch individuals in a manner that will get them to think, feel, and give.

There is an art to fundraising today, and it can become very complex, complete with software, advanced communications systems, marketing strategy, and corporate grant proposals, but at the root of it all is the same basic need—to raise money for your cause, whatever that may be. Keep in mind that the most comprehensive fundraising software program or websites still have not matched the success of eighty-plus years of Girl Scout cookie sales.

It is important, therefore, to take a simplified approach to raising funds, no matter how creative or complex your upcoming fundraising plan may be. We, therefore, take a practical, hands-on approach that can meet the needs of both the multimillion-dollar nonprofit organization and the local twenty-two-member PTO. After all, within the certain boundaries, there are no "right" or "wrong" means of fundraising, only the means to which you are successful at reaching your goal or goals.

The key to successful fundraising is not really whether you sell wrapping paper or scented candles, it's your inner desire to make a difference. If you have a passion and can convince others that you are working for a worthwhile cause, be it fighting domestic violence, to find a cure for Alzheimer's disease, or save the whales, then other people will be touched and will step forward and pitch in with goods, supplies, volunteer hours, or good old money (funds!).

This book highlights examples of many small-scale fundraising efforts and builds on the theme that fundraising is doable at any level. The focus is at the local level, since fundraising really begins when a child asks his or her mom or dad if he or she will buy candy or wrapping paper to help raise money for the child's school, or when the church opens its doors for a bake sale one afternoon, or when the Cub Scouts offer car washes to the local community. Perhaps that's what is meant by the saying "charity begins at home".

Chapter 1: Basics Of Raising Money

Fundraising can encompass a wide range of possibilities, from raising several million dollars for a new wing to be added to a local hospital or to raise a few hundred dollars for new sports equipment for an elementary school. The idea of fundraising, however, offers a community, school, or organization more than just a means of raising money. It can also provide camaraderie as you work together as a team, a place for individuals to use skills and talents they may not use in their everyday workplace, a lesson in responsibility for young people, and a sense of community.

Your fundraiser may be the starting point for members of your neighborhood to meet other likeminded individuals and start discussing various community issues. It may also be a way of generating support for a cause that you believe in.

Today, it is common to find schools encouraging students from grade school through college to engage in fundraising activities. While the parents could raise substantial amounts of money without the help of their children, these activities provide young people with a sense of teamwork and a lesson in responsibility.

And, of course, there is the personal satisfaction that you get from helping out a cause that you believe in.

Support and Involvement

When a group or organization, whether fraternal, charitable, or political, hold a fundraiser, they take some of the burdens of financial support off of their membership and gain the support of a wider audience. This can help spur public involvement and promote public awareness.

For example, when individuals pledge money to PBS, they are becoming involved, in a small way, in the work of that organization, while also showing support. Not unlike showing up at a stockholders meeting, they can become a small part of something larger. Many people are involved in fundraising for the dual purposes of helping others and socialization. Helping to organize and run the annual carnival at your daughter's grade school not only raises money to help the school, but it's also a great way to meet other parents and get to know more people in the community.

To run a successful fundraising drive or event, you need to introduce your members, volunteers, and everyone involved in the activities to one another. You want to establish a team for a successful fundraising effort.

Good Public Relations

While raising money for a specific goal is the primary objective, be it fighting a disease or building a gymnasium, fundraising objectives also highlight and promote the work of your group or organization. You will find that while promoting a specific fundraising effort, you will also distribute literature and tell others by word of mouth about the goals and mission of your group and the cause behind your fundraiser.

For example, if representatives from the American Heart Association are collecting money at a street fair, they will very likely have fliers and data available to distribute so that the public can learn more about what they do. Also, they will probably provide important health-related news about how to keep your cholesterol levels down and similar information. Fundraising often provides a means of educating the public through providing pertinent information gathered by your organization.

Setting a Goal

Before you can set the wheels in motion, it is important that you, and everyone involved in the fundraising efforts, are clear regarding what the money will be used for. Determining your primary goal can often be the cause for great debate in groups or organizations looking to raise money. You must establish priorities for your organization—does the school need new textbooks more than it needs a new gymnasium?

Establishing priorities requires careful examination of the available data. For example, the purpose of your organization may be to fight the HIV/AIDS epidemic. There are many ways to support this cause—you must look at the data and determine what will allow you to be the most effective. Is there a greater need in your community to

7

raise funds to help HIV/AIDS patients or to give to researchers at a medical facility who is seeking a cure for this dreaded disease?

Preliminary research, polls, and evaluations of existing solutions can help you determine which needs you want to prioritize. Studies in your community may show that money has been pouring into support HIV/AIDS research while little money has been donated to local housing for patients. Research may help you establish and then fine-tune your goals.

Even when the purpose seems obvious, such as raising money following the tragic events of September 11, 2001, make sure you are clear regarding how you see the funds being used. For example, many groups specifically raised funds for the families of the victims, while other groups sent money to help the relief workers at Ground Zero. Still, other organizations raised money to help businesses that were affected by the tragedy.

Having a clear goal not only keeps your organization on track, but it also inspires confidence.

The benefits of setting a specific goal will help your organization structure its fundraising plans. A larger-scale goal such as building a new gymnasium will require a more detailed, larger-scale plan of action. Conversely, the goal of buying new cheerleading uniforms will take on a much smaller itinerary. Nonetheless, the goal needs to be communicated to everyone involved directly and indirectly in the fundraising effort.

Targeting an Audience

It is important to establish and look specifically at your target audience even before planning the details of your fundraising events or activities. Your goal is to raise money, but someone needs to be on the other end of that equation, writing out checks or handing over cash.

Can you profile potential donors? Do you know who will be interested in helping you meet your goal? Can you reach these people?

It is in your best interest to establish who will be donating money for your fundraising project to be a success. It will help you establish the magnitude of the project and determine whether your goal is feasible. If for example, you are going to try to collect funds from the students at the local high school, it is highly unlikely that you are going to raise the cash needed to build a whole new gymnasium. You will need to either establish a fundraising plan that attracts the corporate leaders in your community or scale down your goal to converting the old auditorium into a part-time gymnasium, rather than having a new structure built from the ground up.

One of the biggest downfalls of local fundraisers is not knowing the community. Lofty goals and inappropriate fundraisers are a bad combination. Learn who comprises your target audience, what will attract them to your cause, and whom you may realistically tap for funding.

It is also presumptuous to expect everyone on campus or in the neighborhood to get involved and donate money. A large, high-profile organization such as the Red Cross has arms that can extend nationwide and even worldwide. They can expect a large return based on calculating the percentages and maintaining a database showing them how many people donate money annually. The majority of local fundraising efforts have neither such a database to work from nor such a far-reaching network. Therefore, you are well advised to do some preliminary research and look into the potential donor base for your project.

If for example, you are raising money for a sports program for underprivileged kids, you might want to tap into the local athletes and sports enthusiasts in your area. Studies show that women will more readily donate to a school-based, education-related fundraiser than men will. College students have been known to have a greater passion for environmental and ecological concerns. Minorities have a greater concern for social and human rights issues. It is to your advantage to seek out such data before your fundraiser.

Rallying Some Troops

"I wish I could, but I'm just too busy." That's a phrase you will hear all too often when trying to rally troops to work on your fundraising efforts. Everyone feels pressed for time, and you may feel like it's hard to find people willing to carve out time in their schedules to work with you. But there are many people out there who will be ready to give some time and effort to support a good cause. You just have to find them.

Reasonable Goals

Set goals that you can reach. This may seem obvious, but it is important that you consider how much work can reasonably be accomplished by the number of volunteers you have.

It is also very important that you rally people behind the idea in a positive, but not pushy, manner. You need to gather prospective team members and promote the reasons behind the need for funding. Also, you want to emphasize the idea of FUNdraising, or having a good time.

It is estimated that more than 75 percent of people involved in fundraising activities are in some manner touched personally by the cause or need to raise funds. From having a sister with kidney disease and joining the Kidney Foundation to simply enjoying the programming on PBS, most people donate time or money to a cause that they have a personal connection to.

Getting others involved in a fundraiser can be very easy if the cause, or need, is obvious and touches the members, students, or community personally. The less well informed your audience is, the more you need to be prepared. Gathering facts and figures isn't very difficult if you utilize the library, town records, and the Internet.

Show them!

A simple example of winning over an audience with research and presentation comes from a young father of two young children, who went before a local town board in his New England community to propose a fundraiser for new and better playground facilities. Many of the people sitting before him were elders and had no idea what, if anything, was wrong with the current playground. His idea didn't get off the drawing board.

Nonetheless, this concerned father persevered, and at the next town meeting, he had documented proof of several injuries that had been sustained by youngsters as a result of the old equipment. To enhance his argument, he brought in visuals in the form of some photographs. In addition to a polished proposal with facts and figures to back up his request, he also brought with him a few of the local kids, including one whose arm was in a cast from a nasty fall off a wobbly set of monkey bars. Sure enough, the town was now behind him and offered their assistance for his fundraising efforts.

A more complex example might be when a "low profile," somewhat obscure illness needs research for funding. Putting together a fundraising dinner might mean presenting the need to raise funds for such an illness to a medical community that has been hard-pressed to stretch their efforts for research to prevent other diseases. Your presentation will need to explain the importance of researching this illness.

You should prepare appropriate literature that supports your fundraising goal or goals. Such literature should illustrate your mission to potential contributors and volunteers. It should also address the urgency behind your goal and the history or background of your group, association, organization, school, or other affiliation. Remember that the people collecting the money, which includes you and your volunteers, also need to present themselves most credibly in your presentation.

Formulating a Plan

Many different elements factor into how you choose a fundraising event. Your fundraiser will become a project, and, not unlike starting a business, it will need to grow and incorporate the skills of various people whom you believe can help you reach the goal.

11

Individuals give over $150 billion per year, or 75 percent, of all contributions to charitable organizations, according to Giving USA, the publication of the American Association of Fundraising Counsel. Foundations, bequests, and corporations combined give the other 25 percent.

You will need to coordinate a time frame because an open-ended project is not a project at all but a process. While established fundraising organizations will always be accepting donations, a specific fundraiser is just that—specific—with a time frame that indicates when sales or services end and totals are added up. Part of your goal will be to raise money to complete such a project by the desired date. The date may be selected for you by the nature of the project. For example, a fundraising drive to buy Christmas presents for underprivileged children will necessarily be time sensitive. Similarly, political fundraisers are planned around the calendar and with the election date in mind.

You will also find that, when starting the wheels in motion for a fundraising project, it is very likely that your school, group, association, organization, or company has done something before to raise funds for a project. Therefore, you need not reinvent the wheel. While you are planning something unique that will achieve this particular goal, you can get rough ideas from project outlines that may already be sitting in your files.

In the end, there are a lot of elements that you will need to consider in your plan. Ask yourself the following questions:

- What is the primary need for funding?

- How much money are you looking to raise?

- Who will be donating the funds? (Or what is your target audience?)

- Who can you rally around yourself to help put this plan together?

- What is your time frame?

Utilize project-planning software or simply get a notebook and start writing ... and be prepared to cross out, erase, delete, or edit often, as even the simplest garage sale advertisement may require numerous revisions.

Honing and Presenting Your Plan

Your initial plan, or idea, will be shaped as you research the need for fundraising in greater detail. However, your idea won't become a full-fledged "plan" until you have gained support from your organization, membership, student body, or association. Unless you can pull off a fundraising activity on your own, you will need to convince others to come on board with you, and listen to their input and suggestions.

Your idea needs to take shape and tell a short story. Remember, you need to rally internal support for the basic fundraising plan before you can start talking about the details and fleshing out the plan. It is essential that your cohorts, be they friends, fellow students, or club members, feel the same sense of passion for your cause as you do on a practical and emotional level. Sometimes this is very easy, as your organization is already dedicated to a specific cause, such as a foundation to fight diabetes.

Don't fill in all the blanks. Make your initial fundraising plan one that captivates and draws attention to your issue. However, you should leave room for other people to provide their ideas. It's much easier to get people to join a work in progress than to try to fit them into predetermined positions simply.

First, be ready to pitch or present your plan. This can be an informal pitch to a small group of fellow students or a prepared statement in front of the board of a long-standing 5,000-member nonprofit organization.

Second, be prepared to answer questions. How much money will we need to raise to build a new roof? Do we have a liaison to help us distribute the funds and any donated items to the local homeless population? Who will we hit up for funds? Your answers should be based on your research.

After you've presented the problem that exists, present your specific plan to solve it. Show the group what your organization will be able to do specifically to make a difference. Here's where you'll tell them what your project is—replacing old textbooks, donating money for medical research, or funding a soup kitchen.

You may need a show of hands to let you know how many people are with you, or a vote by the board to, say, move forward to the next step ... which would likely answer the question, what type of fundraiser did you have in mind? We explore some of your answers to that pressing question below.

Are you excited to work hard?
Congratulations, you are an entrepreneur. The hustle and hard work are now your way of life.

Ideally, I could help you find a button on some website that you could press, and have money come out of your computer like the bank ATM. Unfortunately; I don't know any such magic button. Even if I did, I'd probably keep that magic button all to myself. I would just press that button myself over and over, laughing all the way to the bank. In fact, maybe I already do that. You will never know.

For everyone who doesn't know of such a magic button, raising money is almost always a 100% opposite process: pure hustle.

With almost every strategy we'll cover, there will be one theme: if you sit back and wait for money to come to you, that fundraising strategy won't work. If you hustle, work hard, be resourceful, creative and persistent, money will eventually come. I need you to get this because precisely this point will make all the difference.

I know what you just thought. You thought something like "I am motivated and excited. I'm ready to work hard and hustle and blah blah blah." Excitement is good. You should be excited, but in the beginning, everyone is highly motivated, excited, and says that they will work hard. But business and fundraising isn't a sprint. It is more of a marathon that has many sprints in it. Business is like a sport where there are nearly no rules, and every once in a while someone blindsides you with a club, despite which you have to keep moving forward. Talk to me about your excitement in a year or two. For now, put these words into your mental pocket: persistence, consistency, creativity, resourcefulness, scrappy, hard work, work-life balance.

Just kidding about work-life balance. I got you there, didn't I? Work-life balance is for later. In the beginning, you better be all hustle, my friend. Hustle will be a theme throughout this book. It has to be. If I told you that it would be easy to raise money, I would be lying and painting a false picture. Instead, I am giving it to you straight.

Hope you are still excited because it would be sad if the excitement waned before finishing the first chapter!

Chapter 2: Fundraising for a Non-Profit Organisation

The very first thing that you have to do before you start your fundraising is to do your research. Your goals need to be realistic and obtainable. Write out all your goals and then even see if you can write out any pros and cons there would be to starting the nonprofit organization or to donating funds to the local charity.

This would be kind of like writing out your business plan, but only you're writing out the goals that you want to obtain, and you're also placing your ideas down on paper for you actually to see.

Here are some topics to ask yourself when doing your research.

- Is there a need for this kind of organization?
- Is there another organization already doing what I wish to do?
- Are my goals obtainable?
- What all do I need to have to start this organization?
- How quickly will this organization grow?

A good way to do this is to sit down and write your mission statement. What are you trying to achieve? Your mission statement should describe what it is you are trying to achieve.

Why does this organization exist?

The question is a tough one, but if you can answer that, then you are well on your way to starting up your nonprofit organization. Again, if you can answer that and find that other organizations already meet these needs, then perhaps you should think of joining them in their mission. This doesn't have to be a brand new idea either; you can take an idea that has already started and just place your twist on it. For example, if you want to help children, then find something that is not being done to help out with children.

While writing your mission statement, try and include values that will guide how your nonprofit will operate, primary benefits and services to clients, how you'd like others to view your nonprofit, and groups of clients who will benefit from these services. These should be included so that others know what the mission of your organization is as well as those that are working with you, know how to help you stick to your mission. This is important because you are going to live by your mission statement. This mission statement is going to be the entire object that you base your organization on. It is going to be how you make an impact.

Just make sure that you are clear and concise about what it is that you want. Don't leave any room for any confusion. If there are parts that even you are confused about, go back and rewrite your mission statement. Run your mission statement by other people to see if they are confused about anything. It is best to use simplified words so that your mission statement is easy to understand by all.

Another part of the study process is to figure out what kind of nonprofit you want to start. Do you just want it to be you and a few friends? Something like this would be something like starting a self-help group in your community. This nonprofit is called an informal non-profit. The outreach is small, but there is still an impact to those who are in need. Even in doing a small self-help group, there is the possibility that you are going to end up getting bigger than just one small self-help group. If you and your fellow nonprofit organization helpers are wanting to, you can start several self-help groups in different areas of your local area so that those who cannot travel as far will be able to attend the meetings if they want to.

Do you want your nonprofit to continue after you're gone? If that is the problem, then you may want to begin thinking of incorporating your nonprofit. In doing this, you are making sure that it exists as a separate legal organization. This ensures that it will continue that the nonprofit will continue on its own, have its property as well as its bank account, and will even protect you personally from liability. Just keep in mind that if you incorporate your nonprofit, you may be required to have a board of directors.

A board of directors is a group of people who will oversee the activities of your organization and help you make decisions. The board of directors is kind of like a sounding board. Instead of making any decisions on your own, you will have a group of people you can go to and get their opinion. In some organizations, the board of directors make the final decisions. If someone is no longer qualified to work for the organization, the board of directors will be the final group to decide if that individual can stay with the organization or is going to be terminated.

As with anything, there will be taxes. Talk to an accountant or the IRS to determine whether or not your nonprofit should be tax exempt or if it will qualify for tax deductions. Both of these statuses will depend on the nature of your organization as well as the services that are offered. If you work off of donations, there may be the possibility that you will be able to receive tax deductions for those donations.

Two last things that you need to research are, does your organization need a fiscal sponsor? And, do you need a lawyer? A fiscal sponsor will help get you started by sponsoring you because you don't have the sufficient resources to handle the startup costs and fees that come with starting a nonprofit organization. Not only will they help with the costs and fees associated with starting your organization, but they can help you gain the skills needed to manage the finances for your nonprofit. Essentially, a sponsor is a more established nonprofit organization that will help you grow into the role of being a non-profit. This is also called networking, and the possibility that you and this other organization work together is going to be likely.

Do not take this organization for granted and go to them for everything. Learn things on your own so that you can make your mistakes and learn from them. If you are unsure if the mistake is going to be detrimental to your organization, then you need to go to your fiscal sponsor and see what they think as well as consulting your board of directors.

Now that you've done all this work, you're going to want to protect it and yourself. A non-profit lawyer will be able to help you with protecting all the hard work that you've put into starting your nonprofit.

Any and all fees associated with starting up your organization need to be paid. There is the possibility that your local or state government will have fees associated with you keeping your non-profit open. This is where having a lawyer and accountant will come in handy. A lawyer will alert you of these fees and let you know what the money is going towards; while an accountant will help you to make sure that the fees get paid to keep your organization open.

An accountant will also be beneficial in making sure that you keep your non-profit's bank account by the guidelines that are required for you to follow.

Fundraising

You have started your non-profit!! After all that research, you finally got the mission statement down, people who are going to work for you, a fiscal sponsor who is going to help you learn how to manage your finances and is going to help you with some of the start-up costs. Not to mention you have turned in all your forms to the IRS after sending them to your lawyer and making sure that they were all in line with what is required for a non-profit. At this point, you probably even have a board of directors that is there to help make sure you don't make any business decisions that could end up getting your organization closed. Everything seems good up to this point. But, where are you going to get money to keep your nonprofit running?

This is where fundraising comes into play.

Event fundraisers involve getting donations of goods that you're going to auction off, supporters to help with entertainment, food, drinks, the event staff, the publicity, location, invitations, so on and so forth. All these are just part of what is needed in making sure that you have a successful event. Make sure that when you are planning an event, you are keeping your goals obtainable just as you did when you were first researching how to start your organization.

If this is your first event, keep it smaller so that you can see how it works out before making it a big event that everyone is sure to love. But, when starting with the smaller event, try out different ideas that you come up with to see if you can get donors or to see what your guests like and don't like. It is better to attempt to try out new ideas on a smaller group of people rather than to do something that could cost you a lot more money in the end.

Another idea is to hold several small event fundraisers throughout the year that are set in place in advance so that the attendees know what to expect. Many attendees are repeaters because they believe in what the organization stands for and want to continue to share their support in some way, so they come to the events that are hosted by the nonprofit organization.

A big thing that you need to keep in mind with an event fundraiser is the timeline of the event. Don't put off any of the planning until the last minute or else the fundraiser will not be as successful as you wish it to be. If you've picked a theme for your event, make sure that you don't have some obscure decorations that have nothing to do with the planned theme. Keep it all decent and possibly even simple. Don't put a negative view on your organization or it could be hard in the future.

If you do not have a large collection of staff that you can delegate tasks out to or pay, you can also do a product fundraiser. These are good for clubs with members or church congregations. Consider the types of fundraisers that schools do, but with different products.

One good idea would be selling pretzels, for example. Many people like pretzels and you can run a fundraiser like this for several weeks so that you can gain as many orders as possible. Don't limit it just to your local area either. Have your members reach out to their friends, family, co-workers, or anyone else who may be willing to help in making your fundraiser a success. A way that you can even reach out to the community is to set up a booth outside of a local supermarket that will allow you to sign up people willing to "donate" to your cause.

If you do not want to do food, you can also do a fundraiser using candles or any other various objects. A good idea is to make sure that it is something that people buy year round and can even give as a gift. Many people use fundraisers as a way to shop for presents for birthdays, anniversaries, and holidays as well as being supportive of a charity or nonprofit organization. Make sure that anything you decide to do a fundraiser on is small and of good quality as well as being affordable.

There will be costs associated with any fundraiser such as getting the items to the location and even paying the company in which the items are coming from, but the fees for these will not come out of your own pocket, they will work with you and their fees will be included in their price. The only thing that you need to make sure of is that you get enough orders for the price to possibly be lowered on the shipping and handling. Everyone has money difficulties. Keep this in mind, would you want to spend that much on that object? If you wouldn't, then why have someone else do it?

Just like with anything, there are rules to being able to fundraise for a nonprofit organization. If you do not work within these rules, then there is a chance that your organization can be fined, you could lose your status as a nonprofit organization or even be closed down.

One of the first things that you need to do is to fill out a Unified Registration Statement (URS). This form is to help collect all the data that is required for any nonprofits that are performing charitable solicitations within their jurisdictions. If your state accepts the URS, it can be used there as your registrations. Your nonprofit will be subject to the registration laws of any and all states that you are performing any charitable solicitations in.

The few states that do not take the URS are Florida, Oklahoma, and Colorado. In these states, you will be required to fill out the state forms. There is the possibility in these states that you will be required to write a check for any registration fees while adding in the proper forms and mailing them into the administering agency. Do not just assume that there are no fees or forms to fill out because you live in a state that does not accept the URS. In doing this, you will be putting your organization in danger of being closed down.

Just like with anything there are certain rules that you must follow. When holding a fundraiser, you don't want to hire a firm to run your fundraiser for you because the firm will hold back some of the money to pay for all the expenses that they had to put out to deal with hosting the event. The percentage that goes to the firm that can be as high as 90% while only 10% of what comes in from the fundraiser will go to your cause.

How would you feel if you gave your money to a nonprofit that you firmly believed in only to find out that a small percentage of your money is going to that organization? If you wouldn't tell your attendees about everything, then why do it?

The entire point of fundraising is to put money towards what your cause is, don't spend money on things that take money away from your cause. The whole purpose of starting your nonprofit organization was to bring your cause to a new light and to be able to make a change for your cause.

Keep track of your spending because, at the end of the year, you have to be able to explain where all the money went that you spent. When doing the taxes to keep the tax exemption or tax deduction that your organization has gotten from the IRS, every donation, every dollar that comes into the nonprofit has to be accounted for to make sure that you are not claiming a nonprofit status when you are a for-profit organization.

There is also the local business around your non-profit that may be willing to donate to your organization. A lot of businesses have an amount set aside that goes towards charitable giving. Some businesses can give more than others due to revenue, but they are always willing to try and help if it is within their budget. Even if they cannot help financially, they are almost always willing to put up fliers for events that you may be having later on.

Chapter 3. Fundraising Ideas

Some of the following ideas are aimed at those in the US, and others at those in the UK, but the general principles can be used in any country around the world. In this chapter, there are close to 100 fundraising ideas!!

Books

You can buy cheap books and sell them for a profit. You can purchase box sets of books from discount book companies and then sell the books individually at a higher price to make a profit. Make sure you pass on some of the discounts to your supporters, parents and the public as then they will be pleased and will purchase books from you again in the future. You could also contact publishers regarding any stock they are planning to get rid of. They often sell this stock at rock bottom prices or will give it away for free, so ask to be added to their mailing list regarding any old or discounted stock. It is also great publicity for the publisher as they are then linked to a charitable or fundraising cause. And it doesn't have just to be children publishers – contact local history publishers and fiction presses to see what is available.

Get a website

It goes without saying how important the Internet is for marketing, spreading awareness and general communication on what you are doing and events being planned, so it is essential that you acquire a professional looking website. However, this doesn't have to be expensive or difficult! Many companies offer professional templates for you to use and start at less than £20 a year, including your domain name and email addresses. Just search 'cheap/ free website templates' in google, or something similar. By having a website, you can keep supporters up to date on activities and events being planned as well as any financial targets you are aiming for. Make sure you utilize your 'meta-tags' fully so that people can find you on search engines such as Google and Yahoo.

Internet purchases

Register at www.easyfundraising.org.uk or a similar website and encourage your supporters to go to this site when buying from their favourite online retailers. It doesn't cost your supporters any extra by doing this, but your charity or school will receive cash back payments up to 15% of whatever has been bought by your supporters, with no catch to you and no catch to the consumer. Why not recommend your supporters have this website as their homepage, so they don't forget to just click on it first before they go off and do their online shopping? Also, make sure you promote this at key times of the year – well before Christmas to remind people as well as Mother's Day and Father's Day.

Presidents Day or Washington's birthday

(The third Monday of February)

Have a sponsored Presidents of the USA quiz, make and sell American food, make American flag tea towels or coasters for people to buy and even have an American line dancing and music evening!

Harvest festival

(Can be anytime in autumn)

Similar to the USA's Thanksgiving, this is a celebration to give thanks for the reaping and gathering of grain. Celebrate it by selling handmade corn dolls (made from a harvested sheaf of corn) with people donating food that can be distributed to the needy. Some people even hold a scarecrow festival, with a competition to find the best scarecrow!

Buy and sell

Sometimes it isn't always possible to make things in advance or during your event or even to ask for donations. Sometimes you need to buy items at a discounted price and sell them on for a profit. There are many items you can purchase that can be connected to your charity, society, club or school, either branded with your logo or linked to the theme of your event. Following are just some suggestions of buying in bulk and selling on to the public and your supporters for a profit.

Branded merchandise

Anything can be branded with your logo and aim (mugs, pens, t-shirts, coasters, tea towels, bags) and can be sold at a marked up price at your event for a profit. Ensure that no dates are included and that any branding isn't specific to one event, so if the items don't sell at that particular Summer Fair or your autumn fundraising event, they can always be sold at Christmas or in the New Year.

Rubber wristbands

This is a popular and contemporary fundraising item that can be bought in bulk in a variety of colours (or one colour connected to your charity, society, club or school) with your charity's name or logo printed on. They can be sold as an accessory for people to wear and show their support or can even be sold as part of an entry ticket to your charity, school or village event, with the cost of the rubber wristband included in the entry price.

Plant sale

Buy plants at a wholesaler or cost from your local garden centre and sell them for a marked up price at your spring fair. You could ask your local plant nursery if they could create an order form that you can distribute to parents, parishioners and supporters. Once the orders and money have been taken, your charity, society or school receives a percentage of the profits made. You could do this throughout the year: spring bulbs, summer flowers, autumn colours and even Christmas trees. Alternatively, ask a local garden centre to set up a stall at your event with a percentage of takings donated to your charity.

A rose for 'Rosie.'

If you are borrowing money for a children's charity or hospice, then why not personalise it by using one of the children's names (if it is the same as a name of a flower) and associating it with a gift? You could buy cut up roses from a flower wholesaler or florist, wrap it in some lovely cellophane and ribbon and then sell it at a marked up price – 'A rose for Rosie'! You could also use this for lilies, daisies and poppies. This works wonderfully for spring and summer events as well as for Mother's Day. It also creates a lovely personal touch to your fundraising that the local press will probably like to cover in a feature.

Toys

If you contact a local manufacturing company of toys and explain what you are doing (i.e. raising money for your charity, school, club or society) they are likely to sell you a bulk quantity of toys at a substantial discount in return for publicity about their toys. You can then sell the toys for a marked up price (but still less than the recommended retail price, so passing on some of the discounts to your supporters) at your fundraising event or direct through an order form. You could also consider contacting your local toy shop to see if they can do something similar. The good thing about toys is that they don't go out of date and there are always new children joining your club, society, school or church and attending your fundraising events for the first time. If you are borrowing money for a children's hospice, you could try and purchase a toy that has a personal or significant meaning for the children you are supporting, such as a sensory toy like a kaleidoscope or a musical toy. If you are raising money for your school, then you can choose an educational toy or something that is linked to the curriculum.

Balloons

A very simple item you can buy and then sell at your event are balloons. Either shiny, big helium ones or just standard air ones, attached to some string. It is very cheap to run, and if you don't price them too expensive, they will sell well to children and parents. If you don't have enough volunteers to sell balloons at your event, then tie them to the gazebos or table legs of your stalls. Not only will it brighten up the whole event but it also means the person selling cakes or running a lucky dip stall can also sell a few balloons. You could even get balloons printed with your charity, school, club or society name and logo on. Just like other items, don't mention one event or date on the balloon to ensure any unsold balloons can be used again at future events.

Tuckshop/penny sweets

A sweet shop is a great way of people using up their spare change and keeps children quiet for a minute or two. You can sell crisps and cans of pop, bought in bulk from a local wholesaler, and if you buy tubs of sweets and paper bags, you can make up little bags of sweets in advance to the value of 20p and 50p. As sweets have a long shelf life, any sweets not sold at your first event can be sold again at your next one.

Themes and events

The following gives examples of all the different events and themes you can run throughout the year. Remember that at each event organised you could sell a programme (which includes local advertising inside), sell drinks and food, play games, ask for donations, have a raffle and so much more. Here is a list of seasonal events (arranged by date from 1st January to 31st December) and suggestions for various activities you could run:

Burns Supper

(25th January)

Enjoy the poetry of the great Scottish Robert Burns with some haggis, whiskey and a recital of Burns' unforgettable poetry. You could wear a kilt for the day in the office, run a 'design your own tartan' competition or have an evening of Scottish music and dancing.

Australia Day

(26th January)

On a cold, wet and possibly snowy winter's day in January, wear beach shorts in the office and hold a barbeque outside. Or have a sponsored boomerang contest, learn the didgeridoo or have an orienteering contest to find the kangaroo. For schools, why not do a sponsored 'Facts about Australia' contest and maybe contact a school in Australia who children can write to?

Chinese New Year

(Late January – mid-February)

Sell Chinese food, performed Chinese folklore with dancing dragons, sell fortune cookies and beautiful lanterns, make and sell bookmarks with Chinese writing on and even have a sponsored great wall of China walk on a treadmill.

Japan's National Day

(11th February)

Sell sushi and sashimi, wear a kimono all day, have a sponsored sumo costume race or contest in inflatable sumo suits, run a sponsored Japanese endurance challenge, have a sponsored Mount Fuji climb on a treadmill, or even hold your Japanese tea ceremony followed by some karaoke! You could even make and sell origami paper cranes, personalised Japanese bookmarks or door signs or even Japanese face painting.

Valentine's Day

(14th February)

Sell roses, origami paper hearts, fairy cakes decorated with hearts on top or hold Valentine's disco, find the Queen of Hearts game or how about a speed dating night? Why not consider organising a sponsored 'hug-a-thon' or the largest group hug?

Shrove Tuesday / Pancake Day

(46 days before Easter)

It has to be everything to do with pancakes on this day! Pancakes (or crepes) to make, sell and eat with lots of different fillings: sweet fillings such as lemon and sugar, jam or chocolate, or savoury ones such as cheese, ham and mushrooms. Why not have a pancake and frying pan race followed by a sponsored pancake toss?

St David's Day

(1st March)

Celebrate Wales with lamb and leek cuisine, sell bunches of daffodils, learn some Welsh place names for a geography test, or sponsor people to climb Snowdonia. If you can't get to North Wales to climb Snowdonia, then why not have a sponsored climb on a step machine?

St Patrick's Day

(17th March)

Everybody loves St Patrick's Day: a great day to enjoy all things Irish – Guinness, whiskey, Irish music, Irish dancing! Why not put on your own Riverdance show, wear nothing but green for the day or even write your limericks for an Irish literary night?

Easter Fair

(A moveable date but usually between March and April)

A popular one for children with a hunt the Easter Egg game, an Easter egg tombola, a visit from the Easter Bunny, egg decorating, an egg roll down a hill race and you mustn't forget the egg and spoon race! You could also put on a play about the Easter story (selling programmes, food and refreshments plus a raffle during the interval) or how about a sponsored 'quit it' for the whole of Lent - maybe coffee, sweets or chocolate. You might even encourage someone to stop smoking!

St George's Day

(23rd April)

As this is England's national day, why not have a medieval England theme and a 'galloping knight race' (i.e. on a pogo stick or using a decorated mop or broom)? Dress up in medieval costume for the day, sell red and white cakes, find the Knight in a pack of cards game (like the Queen of Hearts game on page 34), and maybe have an old English poetry recital with some Morris dancing?

South Africa's National Day

(27th April)

Celebrating South Africa's first democratic general election in 1994, why not use this event to highlight charities in Africa and human rights? Have a sponsored silence or fast, climb up Table Mountain (on a treadmill) and sell South African food such as biltong, boerewors and redbush tea. You could also run a 'facts about South Africa' test.

May Day

(1st May)

The first of May is a great time to have a village fete or a community gathering, selling cakes and drinks alongside lots of lovely outdoor activities for everyone to either watch or participate in. You could dance around a Maypole, put on a play and maybe have a 'balloon release' race (page 32).

Queen of England's birthday

(1st or 2nd Saturday in June)

Just like the previous entry, have a truly British fundraising event on the Queen's birthday, selling teas, sandwiches and scones followed by a sponsored quiz on the Kings and Queens of England and the United Kingdom.

Mothers Day

(Different date in each country)

Fundraise by having an event that celebrates motherhood. Put on a play, sell flowers, have a pampering evening with an external company (you receive a share of the profits from any beauty items sold at the event) or even get the children to do a sponsored 'washing-up and tidy bedrooms' for a week! You could also create personalised stone paperweights, bookmarks, origami hearts or bracelets for people to buy for their Mum.

Father's Day

(Different date in each country)

Celebrate fatherhood by organising a sports outing to football, rugby, cricket, motor racing or horse racing event (the coach and entry fee included in a ticket price, which also raises a small profit for your charity). Alternatively, organise sporting activities, selling food and drinks and running lots of sporting challenges finishing with an arm-wrestling contest!

Canada Day

(1st July)

A great Canadian event that could be decorated in red and white maple leaf flags and balloons. Sell waffles and maple syrup, have a sponsored hike as a Rocky Mountain ranger or a sponsored lake swim or how about a grizzly bear tea party?

France Day

(14th July)

A wonderful continental day that could include a sponsored speak French for 24 hours, a sponsored bike ride like the Tour de France, sell croissants and French food, perform a play about a particular period in French history or dress all day as a stereotypical or famous French person!

Sport's Day

(July)

Whether your fundraising is connected to a school or not, a sports day for children or a 'retro sports day' for adults is great fun! Run traditional school races such as the egg and spoon race, the sack race and the three-legged race. Sell drinks and food as well as put on a variety of stalls to keep spectators entertained, including a raffle and some bean bag sports activities (see page 42 for ideas).

Summer Fairs

(Anytime in July/August)

Celebrate the summer with a glorious fair. Bunting, bouncy castles, funny races, face painting, homemade lemonade, pony rides and lovely food to eat such as strawberries and ice-cream. For adults, why not put on a 'play in the park', a sponsored walk or cycle (that ends at the fair) or a 5km run around the parameters of the fair?

India's Independence Day

(15th August)

A great excuse to make and sell some wonderful curries, naan bread and poppadoms! Have some traditional Indian dancing for entertainment, wear a sari all day, have an 'Indian' quiz night (while serving the curry!) and maybe arrange a performance or a play about an Indian religious story.

Spain's National Day

(12th October)

Serve up paella and tapas, have a Spanish music and flamenco night, make Spanish fans to sell and have a sponsored 'bull-fight' with someone pretending to be the bull!

Halloween

(31st October)

A spooky yet fun event! Hold a 'Halloween disco' for children or adults, wear fancy dress for the day, sell pumpkin pie, pumpkin soup and ghost shaped biscuits.

Bonfire night / Guy Fawkes night

(5th November)

I love this event! It is one of my favourites! The smell of toffee apples, treacle toffee and parking; the sounds and lights of a firework display and bonfire. Why not put on a Guy Fawkes play or organise a history quiz about it? And don't forget 'A Penny for the Guy'!

Thanksgiving

(The fourth Thursday in November)

Offer a feast of food to paying guests to give thanks and put on a play about the Pilgrim Fathers. You could even hold the States of America or a Presidents of America quiz.

St Andrew's Day

(30th November)

Scotland's national day, so why not serve haggis, have a whiskey tasting session, wear a kilt for the day, toss the caber and hold a céilidh?

Plays

Why not put on a play? Not only do you get money from your ticket sales, but also for any refreshments and programmes (including advertising) sold during the interval. You can also hold a raffle on the night of the performance (drawn in the interval or at the end).

Talent show

Alternatively, hold a local talent contest with singers, magicians, comedians and bands. Advertise for a variety of acts (with a cash prize as an incentive), charge an entry fee for spectators or ask for donations and you can have a great deal of fun as well as raise money from the sale of refreshments and programmes.

Concert

Put on a concert. You never know what hidden talents your colleagues and friends might have! If you are part of a choir, then put on the performance, wonderful at any time of the ear but especially lovely at Christmas time. Tickets could be sold in advance or at the door as well as the usual programmes, refreshments and other games.

Music night

Alternatively, pay someone to put on a concert or a music night. Tribute bands can be great fun as well as draw in a big crowd, from whom you can collect donations, sell refreshments and have other activities and games on at the same time. You could also organise a decade night (such as the 1970s, 1980s, a rock n roll night or the swinging sixties). Choose a decade, pick music to suit and then encourage people to come in fancy dress. Tickets can be sold in advance or at the door, as well as food and drinks during the evening plus a few extra games (raffle, the best fancy dress costume etc.). For a more relaxed music night, why not have a night dedicated to one particular genre (opera, jazz, blues or musicals) with a band and food?

Battle of the bands

Why not run your mini-Glastonbury with a competition between local bands to see who the best is (voted for by the audience)? Money can be raised from entry tickets, the sale of food and refreshments as well as a variety of stalls surrounding the stage.

Award ceremonies

A school or society (such as a dance club, gymnastics club or swimming club) could hold an award ceremony every year, with the sale of refreshments and programmes raising money to support your fundraising activities. At the award ceremony, you could give the winners certificates and medals as well as put on a swimming demonstration, ballet performance or school recital to all the proud parents.

Street party

Don't wait for the next royal coronation or wedding and have your street party to support your local hospice, school or charity. With colourful bunting decorating the neighbourhood, a wide variety of stalls, games and refreshments, not only will you create a great community atmosphere but you will also raise valuable funds for your local charity or organisation.

Local festivals/community fairs

If the above is too hard to organise, then why not have a stall or two at a local fair or festival? Homemade cakes and refreshment stalls do particularly well, but why not consider an awareness stall about your charity and sell branded merchandise? Alternatively, offer fun games for people to try for a donation and promote the work that is done by your charity or society.

Dinner dance

These are a very popular ticketed event that can raise a lot of money – however, they do require quite a lot of organising and promotion to ensure you get enough people attending. While having the dinner or the dance, why not run some other activities, such as a raffle or the 'heads and tails' game?

Dancing/disco

A night of dancing is very popular, and tickets can be sold in advance with refreshments, games and other activities available during the evening. Why not try different types of dancing – a Scottish céilidh, Irish dancing, American line dancing, salsa, ballroom? Discos are thoroughly enjoyed by children and can be tagged to other events (such as a Valentine's Disco, a Halloween Bop, a Christmas Shindig). Sell tickets in advance or at the door as well as the usual refreshments and sweets on the night. You could even run party games and a raffle.

Masked ball

For an evening of the utmost glamour, why not organise your very own masked ball? With a fancy dress theme such as Kings and Queens, you could hold your very own Venetian ball with prizes for the best costume, the 'heads and tails' game (page 49) and a raffle.

Karaoke competition

If singing is more popular than dancing, then why not run your karaoke night (on a Japanese themed evening?) or an 'X-Factor' competition with refreshments, games and food on sale? You never know, there could be a star amongst your pupils, society members or charity supporters!

If physical activities are more popular with your supporters than music, dancing and singing, then why not organise a sport themed event, where individuals or teams pay an entry fee to participate, and a cash prize is offered to the winners? It is all about having an attraction that people will come and either watch or participate in, thus raising money and awareness for your charity. Once you have created 'a draw', and you have a crowd of people at your event, you can then raise more funds through a variety of spectator activities (games, food, drinks, raffle, donation buckets, face-painting etc.).

Charity golf day

With the support of a local golf club and the lure of a cash prize plus a possible trophy, you will attract a large golfing crowd who you can then tempt with a range of additional fundraising stalls.

Bowls tournament

Either ten-pin bowling, skittles, or grass bowls – whichever you choose, you can create a strong contest by having either individuals or teams play as part of a knock-out competition.

Football tournament (5 aside)

Create a knock out tournament that can be held over one day – for example, 20-minute games. You can sell personalised t-shirts to the teams, refreshments to the spectators as well as put on a variety of activity and fun stalls to keep everyone entertained. Let's just hope it doesn't go to penalties!

Darts tournament

A darts knock-out competition that can either be played as individuals or teams, with food and games put on for spectators and participators.

Wimbledon

A charity tennis knock-out tournament can be very competitive, whether it is mixed, men, ladies, juniors singles or doubles matches being played. Keep the matches short by just playing one set. Why not also consider a table tennis or badminton tournament? You could also sell iced tea, homemade lemonade and strawberries and cream to the spectators.

Cricket charity contest

As above, but keep games short by limiting the number of bowls thrown. This way more teams can play, and all the games are played on the same day. You could even have a local knockout contest via local villages and raise money for the sale of refreshments, a raffle and activities for the spectators.

If the sport doesn't appeal to your supporters, consider a more cultural event by organising one of the following activities. Money can be raised by an entry fee plus the sale of refreshments:

Gallery or art show

If you have a suitable venue, ask a local art group or artist if they would like to put on a show of their work. You could then sell their artwork and retain a small commission on everything sold at the event for your charity, society, church or school.

Public talks/demonstrations

Every village and town has a plethora of speakers, whether they are local historians, experts in a certain field, travellers, writers or artists. Ask them to support your charity by giving a free talk or demonstration. Tickets could be sold in advance and refreshments sold during the event.

Local historical walk

Ask a local history expert to give a guided walk around your town, city or village. The walk and talk could be free, but refreshments could be sold at the beginning, middle or end of the walk.

Wine tasting evening

This is very popular. Your local wine merchant is likely to offer the wine at a discount as well as recommend a suitable expert. You can make a profit from any wine sold on the night or sell tickets to hear the expert talk about wines from a particular region or how to match wines with certain foods.

Book club

Set up your own book club. While membership to the club will be free, the sale of twenty coffees, teas and snacks every fortnight over a period can add quite a bit to the fundraising account. You could even get local authors to come and give a talk at your club.

Jumble sales & car boot sales

Either charge people an amount per stall at an advertised jumble sale or ask for donations from visitors attending. The sale of refreshments to stall owners as well as customers should also be tapped. Either rent out your car park for a car boot (charging a fee per car and selling refreshments) or invite supporters to bring their cars and donate a percentage of their profits from the event to your charity or cause.

Auction

Ask local companies, shops, business and supporters to donate items for an auction in return for publicity. Make sure you advertise the auction thoroughly in advance to draw in a crowd, promoting the top items being auctioned so that interested people will attend on the day.

Auction of promises

If donations are not forthcoming, donate a particular skill you have or some of your valuable time. An hour's ironing? An afternoon of gardening? A home-cooked meal? A taxi trip into town on a Saturday night? All of these can attract quite a price!

Singles dating night

Why not hold a speed dating night or a single evening? Make it a ticketed event or pay on the door and sell drinks and snacks for the singletons. You could even organise a disco or a meal during the evening. Just think, your fundraising could be the start of some lovely romances!

Magic / Entertainment show

Ask a magician, entertainer or children's entertainer to put on a show for either adults or children for a reduced fee. You could sell tickets, refreshments and promote the work you and your charity, society, club or school are doing. The entertainer would also get considerable publicity as well, as their name is associated with a good cause.

Coffee morning

A simple tea, coffee and cake morning can raise solid funds as well as provide a regular social event for people. People can either pay for any drinks or cakes they purchase or pay a donation on entry which includes a hot drink and sweet treat.

Quiz night – question of sport, university challenge

All you need is a list of general knowledge questions (or themed questions linked to the date the quiz is held on or the causes you are supporting) and a cash prize. Teams pay an entry fee to participate, and refreshments (both food and drinks) are sold on the night too. You could even sell raffle tickets for a draw that can be taken at the interval. The quiz could be held on a themed night, such as the anniversary of Gandhi's birthday (2nd October), and curries could be served at the interval or while the answers are being marked. Quizzes are very popular, and if you promote it well in your local community and amongst your supporters, you can get a good turnout.

Bingo

Bingo nights are great fun and appeal to children as well as to adults! Cards and balls can be bought online, and once you have got them in, they can be used again and again and again and again...! Participators pay an amount per game and prizes are awarded to the first person to shout 'bingo', when all the numbers on their card have been called! The prizes are usually cash prizes but if this is too expensive then consider offering vouchers donated by local businesses in exchange for publicity.

Nature walk

A nature walk (with a local walking guide and refreshments on sale) is a lovely event in all seasons. In fact, the same walk can be done in all four seasons as the difference in nature, wildlife and foliage can be quite distinct. Why not collect leaves or stones along the way and then provide tables for children to decorate them at the end of the walk, or draw around them on pieces of paper, to create a nature file? They could then research the names of the trees the leaves have fallen from. You could also provide paper and crayons for the children (and adults) to do some leaf rubbings to take away with them as a record of an enjoyable day out.

English garden party

With cucumber sandwiches, scones and tea, homemade lemonade and fresh strawberries with cream, this is a delightful summer event where a croquet competition could be played, a puppet show put on for the children and maybe even an English Romantic poet recital.

Craft show

Either a craft show of items already made specifically in advance of the event for purchasing or a craft show that teaches people the basics of basket weaving, embroidery, knitting, watercolours, soap making, candle carving, card marking, origami, flower arranging etc.

Teddy bear's picnic

One for the little ones! For a small fee, invite toddler groups to come for a lovely picnic in your local park with picnic blankets to sit on, little triangle jam sandwiches and juice to enjoy and lots of fun games to play. It is a great way for new parents to come and meet other parents, for friendships to be formed as well as raise money (and awareness) for your worthwhile cause. Remind everyone to bring along a teddy too!

Mr. & Mrs Evening

Compile a list of questions and (along with a sound-proof booth or a separate room) hold a very memorable Mr. & Mrs. evening. After a series of questions and knock-out rounds, the winning couple who knows each other the best wins a prize (preferably a romantic meal donated by a local restaurant). Money can be raised at this event from food and drink sales, the 'heads and tails' game (page 49) and a raffle, along with any donations made or a small minimum donation to take part.

Fashion show

Ask your local clothes store to put on a fashion show with the clothes being shown available to buy during the evening for a discount off the recommended retail price (with a share of the takings donated to your cause). You could also sell refreshments, food and hold a raffle during the event. Alternatively, ask the fashion students at your local college, high school or university to present their work to a paying audience?

Eurovision party

Celebrate the Eurovision Song Contest by having a sweepstake on the winning country as well as those who receive 'null points'! You could even have a disco (to Eurovision music) with a raffle and drinks on sale. Why not encourage participators to come in fancy dress based on the different countries singing with the best costume winning a prize?

Your very own 'Crufts' / pet show

Organise your own 'Crufts' but for all pets not just dogs. Everyone pays an entry fee which goes towards a cash prize for the winners, with more money raised from side-line activities and the sale of refreshments. You could also ask your local pet store to sponsor the event by either providing vouchers or prizes in return for publicity or by being the judge during the event. This is a great fundraising idea if you are raising money for animal welfare causes.

Organise outings / Day trips

Why not organise outings with a local coach company, either to a historic city, the races or attraction? By purchasing admission tickets in bulk and covering the hire of the coach in the ticket price, you can make quite a profit if you sell each ticket for a small profit, as well as create a good social event for your supporters. You can even do a raffle on the coach journey down and sell refreshments and snacks.

Using the Internet

Following are a selection of ideas on how you can make money or raise your profile on the Internet, and consequently gain more supporters locally, nationally and even internationally who can help with your fundraising activities:

Website advertising

Once you have your website, make sure you use it to the maximum with linked web advertising, either with Google Ads or by selling advertising space to local and national businesses connected to your aims. You can also offer exchange adverts with another charity or a related society.

Social networking sites

Establish your charity, society, club or school on social networking sites such as Facebook, Twitter and MySpace to spread awareness of future events you are planning and fundraising targets you are aiming for. You can link your page to other pages and create a wider local, national and international network of supporters. 'Causes' on Facebook is a popular way for individuals and charities to promote awareness of their campaigns. By setting yourself up and spreading the word among current friends and supporters, you will be amazed how quickly your cause will grow in support, which is fantastic for telling people about your aims, targets and forthcoming events.

Write a blog

If you are a keen writer and can write witty, amusing or thoughtful material then start writing a blog on your website. Not only will you keep your supporters up to date on how the fundraising is going, but by writing on the internet, you can start to attract followers from all over the world. While it might not transcend directly into money straight away, a blog is a great way of making the fundraising personal, up to date and interesting.

Online auctions and Ebay

You can sell items on an online auction (such as www.mycharityservices.com or eBay) to raise money for your charity, promoting the auction through your supporters on social network sites such as Facebook and Twitter. Alternatively, you can ask supporters who sell items on eBay whether they could add a donation option to every sale. This way people who buy items from these sellers can choose whether they would like to add a donation to their total purchase price, just a small amount, so it is hardly noticed by them, say fifty pence. Small amounts such as these accumulated over numerous sales over a period can generate a substantial amount for your charity for little or no work whatsoever. You could also ask your friends and family to donate items for you to sell on Ebay

Sell books via Amazon Associates

By registering yourself with Amazon Associates, you can sell books via your website through Amazon. You are not handling any of the books or payment transactions yourself, merely redirecting any potential customers to Amazon, from whom you receive a percentage of any sales made. You can list the books you want on your website, consequently making a 'library of recommended books' that is appropriate to your fundraising cause.

Create and sell an e-book

If you or your supporters are keen writers, then why not write an e-book and put it on your website for people to download for a small charge? It doesn't cost you anything to do, and the majority of the money comes back to you (with just the company processing the payment taking a small percentage such as PayPal). Alternatively, if you are interested in writing a book that raises money for your fundraising cause as well as spread awareness about a particular issue then contact the publishers of this book, Nell James Publishers.

Widgets and Apps

Put the WhatGives!? or Chipin on your Facebook page, website, blog, Twitter or I-phone. It displays your fundraising goal, has a donate button and is easy to share amongst all your supporters and for them to circulate it amongst their friends and family members. All donations are handled via PayPal, making it easy to collect the funds raised.

Online petitions

If you are looking to create an online petition to create awareness or modify a law, then check at one of the following companies (www.petitiononline.com or www.change.org) who create a petition for free and offer advice on circulating it to your supporters and the wider public, thus raising your profile considerably

.

Chapter 4: 10 Tips On Becoming A Better Fundraising Organizer

Tip 1: They're Not Doing You A Favor

While you need to be professional and express thanks to people who choose to contribute, don't act subservient. While people aren't obliged to help you, many participate in charity or fundraising functions for the tax rebates. A little cynical, maybe, but it can be a contributing factor to the reason behind donating, for some people. So, get your mindset to accept that you're not asking for favors. You're only collecting from those who are ready to give back to society. While you may certainly let people feel through your speech and gifts that they're doing society a favor, if your attitude portrays a begging quality, it will limit your effectiveness as an organizer. It could even lead to more doors closing in your face.

Tip 2: You're A Salesperson, Behave Like One

Yes, you read it right. Society doesn't tend to react well to strange people who walk around asking for money, regardless of the cause. So you need to recognize your position – you're a salesperson, and your product is social welfare in the form of a chosen cause. You need to develop the thick skin and perseverance. Don't take no too easily as an answer, but know when to stop pushing. Learn to convince rather than badger or browbeat. Incentives such as a fun time and tax rebates are an effective motivator, and truth be told, guilt trips are likewise effective. You need to know how to use both to your benefit appropriately.

Tip 3: 'Official' Sells Better

Once you've decided on your cause, then the first step is to get in touch with an NGO or relevant organization that deals with furthering that particular cause. Ask them for any official brochures and other such documents and explain that you wish to fundraise on their behalf. While some NGOs prefer direct donations from their contributors, others might help or advise you on how to perform the task better. If you're raising money for your own group's cause, then be sure to have some pamphlet handouts, and certainly come up with some official receipt books so that you can present donors with official receipts for their donations. Official always sells better than someone going door-to-door asking for funds based solely on their word. Regardless of the form your fundraising campaigns take, always give receipts or verification of donations, and keep a careful note of names and amounts so that you can submit detailed information to the organization. It's not uncommon to write thank you letters afterward, especially for larger donations, so you'll want to have the list of names readily available of who exactly donated what amount. Be prepared in advance, so you don't end up jotting them down on the back of a napkin.

Tip 4: Orient Your Fundraising Activities Around Holidays As Much As Possible

People get significantly more philanthropic around the holidays. Use that to your advantage. After all, if someone has a large turkey freshly roasting in their oven and their house is decked out with holiday cheer, most people will feel a tiny pang of guilt saying 'no' to a donation request of $10.

Tip 5: Always Remember Your Goal and Aim High

Regardless of how persistent you need to be to get the necessary donations, even if it's against your nature, remember the reason behind your efforts. In this case, the end justifies the means. People tend to be aggressive when earning for themselves, yet when collecting for others, they suddenly pull back and act more polite, less pushy. So, it's far easier being aggressive when you're doing it to get something you truly want. The cause, therefore, needs to be something you strongly believe in. If you keep that in mind, you'll find yourself far better at convincing others to help out. And if it's not something you believe in, then maybe you should hand over the reins to another member of your organization.

Be sure to aim even higher than any realistic goal. This presents a challenge and elicits a kind of sympathy and willingness from donors to help reach the set goal. On top of that, it will give you a mental boost to push yourself harder. Imagine the feeling of satisfaction and pride when you end up achieving the larger, more difficult goal that you set for yourself, rather than an easy one.

Tip 6: Specifics Sell Better Than Vague Requests

When you've decided on your cause, and contacted the organization that will receive the money, get an idea of the exact activities the money will go towards. For example, if you're raising funds for hungry people or refugees, get an idea of what a donation of $10, $15, $25 and $50 would specifically pay for in their case. Perhaps it will provide bedding, a certain number of meals for one person, or books in the case of schools. Whether you're going from door-to-door or selling a raffle ticket at your fundraiser, place each donation amount in context - "Would you like to buy a $25 ticket to my fundraiser party that would buy a hungry man in Africa three meals a day for two weeks?" You get the picture.

When you use those specifics, they'll be much more likely to donate the exact amount you're hoping for. It doesn't just play on their sympathy but elevates their trust in your process since you've done your homework and sound legitimate and knowledgeable.

Tip 7: Use EVERY Social Media Tactic In Your Arsenal

Social Media is a remarkably powerful tool, and you shouldn't just use it to marshal resources, but to gather more volunteers as well. Someone could simply donate a small knick-knack for a raffle prize or help organize the campaign better. Also, use it to tell the story of your fundraising as it happens. Right from the first step until the last, post everything on the social media venue of your choice. Write about not just what your plans and achievements are, but the motivation behind organizing the fundraiser. Make sure to include the people who have joined up to help you along, as well as individually thank each donor.

Use these tools to weave a visual/textual story that starts with your very first step, catalogs every event, and ends with the final amount raised. Consider ending the story with you handing over a check with the final amount in view, or of the school library full of new books that were purchased, etc.

Tip 8: Don't Shy Away From Your Resources

Apart from using your social media feed and being sales-like in your approach, don't forget your long list of family, relatives, and friends – a rather valuable pool of potential volunteers, donors, marketers, and service-providers. They can help in any way they can, helping with food, catering, gifts, donations, providing contacts to other valuable donors or service-providers like DJs or local celebrities.

Getting support from your inner circle will strengthen your campaign. Use this resource pool as thoroughly as possible if you want to have the best shot at a great first fundraiser. After this, you'll already have a decent working knowledge and outside contacts willing to participate in their venues or services who wish to participate in this sort of thing. And these contacts may be able to provide further networking sources if they're not available. Networking is a key ingredient in successful fundraising. You'd be surprised at the lengths people go to help if you simply get over any apprehension and just ask.

Tip 9: Get Commercial Establishments Involved, Request For Subsidies And Donations In Exchange For Advertising

Local restaurants, supermarkets and smaller stores are often willing to help, especially if you advertise for them during your event. Get them to donate food or provide large discounts on buffets, whatever you need, in exchange for advertising. You then incorporate the business in your social media campaign and sponsor logos on flyers or other material in your fundraising efforts. The more visibility you can offer them, the more likely they are to help you. Once you've gotten even one establishment to sign up, you may find it easier to recruit others since they don't want to miss out on an advertising opportunity that their competitors are using.

Even for a simple lemonade stand - not that I recommend this as a fundraising event – you could approach a local bakery and ask for the donation of a limited amount of cookies, say twenty that cost $1 each in exchange for advertising and a receipt of donation. You can then advertise the stand and thank the bakery in the same post, and offer the cookies at half the price to the first twenty customers who purchase two lemonades in a single order. The same applies to a larger fundraising campaign.

Tip 10: Get Kids Involved as a Volunteer Labor Force

Get in touch with your local Boy Scouts, Girl Scouts, Cub Scouts, 4-H, or a similar organization. Explain your cause and campaign idea and request volunteer help. Since these organizations do offer badges and medals for community work, you may be able to get a significant amount of youth involvement in your campaign. Use them to help you set-up and run the fundraiser, take them along from door-to-door while collecting contributions – or wherever else you need help. You can also offer certificates of participation for extra motivation. Their presence will not only give your efforts more legitimacy, but their brand recognition and overall cuteness may also help you gather more funds.

Use these ten tips to form the backbone to any campaign method you choose, and you'll raise funds far more effectively.

Chapter 5: Special Events

Nonprofit organizations and businesses can utilize the organization of events geared towards raising funds with tremendous success. In this type of funds generation, you organize fundraising events, which aim at the generation of income and creation of awareness of your business or non-profit regarding particular area of work. The reason why the function is termed as a special event is that the attendants not only come to deliver their contributions, they are also oriented to various functions that your organization performs and the event is both income generating on the side of the organization and educational on the side of attendants.

The running of special events might be quite difficult and tedious, and to an extent, it might not achieve great results intended by the organization. However, many special events have been organized with great success and thus to make your special fundraising event a success, you will need to have a clear strategy that is well defined and which the whole event will be organized and run. It is important to mention that the objectives need to be identified so that all events can be properly planned and it runs on particular definite order.

A variety of special fundraising events can be run, and these events vary regarding the objective for running them and possibly the attendance of the people at the event. Enlistment and profile raising events can be organized by the organization, and they will likely attract media attention that will explore the charity work performed by the company. This will in turn help to build your organization's reputation. These events can also be used to promote new services that you have incorporated and offer in your company while at the same time expanding the existing services that your organization offers. Enlistment and profile events can also be used to persuade potential patrons that the organization is worthy of support in carrying out its charity works and at the same time be a platform for recruiting new volunteers since they can be run on a cost-free basis. If this type of event is run properly, it can greatly help to amass financial support from other people, which will be a valuable fundraising venture.

Some special events can also be organized in a bid to raise money for the nonprofit organization directly. These include indoor or outdoor events and even regular dates where people meet specifically for fundraising purposes, and the attendants usually have information beforehand that fundraising shall be carried out on specific dates so that they can prepare their contributions and at the same time they can invite their friends who might be willing to participate in the fundraising activities. To effectively run these events, the organization might need to create a fundraising calendar, which might be distributed to potential attendants and staff like directors so that they can have prior information.

Support of donors towards funds generation in the nonprofit organization is very vital. To do this effectively, the organization can organize special events with the main aim being to acknowledge support from donors who have significantly contributed financially to the organization. This is usually important since simply saying thank you might not be properly appreciative, considering the financial support received, and therefore a public recognition event for the support from the donors can be quite notable.

Therefore, the events can be held in commemoration of a completion of a major activity, as well as recognize and appreciate the tremendous help from donors and volunteers. Besides appreciation, the event can help raise funds through various ways like ticket selling; existing donors continued contribution and even potential donors contributions so that they too can be accorded recognition in the future.

Considerations For Running Special Events

Effective special events need attention to select yet vital aspects that can greatly influence the success of the event. Largely, the events have to achieve three main objectives. The event should be marketable, which means that it should be able to contribute significantly to the increase in visibility of the organization's profile to those people who attend. Notably, the special event should be able to generate sales, and as such, it should be profitable. Since the primary premise behind holding such a function is to raise funds, it would be such a disappointment if the event turns out to derail the organization financially instead of contributing to the escalation of the financial disposition of the organization. It is important to note that you can run the event based on what had worked before in your community by other organizations that carried out prior activities with similar goals of raising funds.

Venues for the activities are very vital and generally, the venue should be suitable but will largely depend on the objectives of holding such an event with a bigger consideration attached to the budget required to finance and run the event. In case a volunteer offers you a venue to host your events, and such venue satisfies your standards, it would be advisable to take up the offer and utilize that. However, planning of the event should be done first since from the planning; you will identify the type of venue suitable for your events.

In some instances, seeking sponsorship for holding of your event might be appropriate, and if so, you need to have a clear and informed idea on how much money you are expecting from sponsors so that you can shape your budget to hold a smooth yet successful function.

Special events are likely to be a great platform for marketing your products and services. This might necessitate the need for promotion services depending on your target market and possible build-up of a new clientele. Featuring celebrities in the events which will likely attend due to their support for your work as the organization can be a big promotional tool which will likely attract a big audience.

Ticket sales are a major consideration that should be given much deliberation and action to ensure that they greatly increase the funds that you will raise. Usually, tickets are sold out to the people who will attend the function. The best method to boost ticket sales is to organize and hold the event in an attractive environment, and then contact readily reachable audience. However, you need to cost your tickets appropriately bearing in mind the different levels of people who will attend due to disparities in their financial incomes.

However successful an event can be organized and run, follow up is paramount and needs to be deeply put into practice by the organization. This can cover actions ranging from having the details of those who attend so that you can contact them at a later date to printing programs of the organization, which will be distributed to those who will attend the event. Make sure that the programs or brochures contain contact details so that the attendants can easily contact you in future and this will help to build a clientele for future support.

Chapter 6: The Donor

A well-established dancer decided it was finally time to ask a longtime supporter for a large gift. She set up a lunch meeting to "Ask." When the donor responded that he did not have enough to give, the dancer swore off making large Asks and did not do another one until I started working with her.

Two very similar small arts organizations in the same city did what so many groups do: rushed to get their one solicitation of the year out right before the end of December, believing that donors need to get those last-minute tax breaks in. Both solicitations arrived in my mailbox on the same day.

I have witnessed large fundraising teams at big organizations insulate themselves from the actual donors. Lots of work is getting done, but very few people are going out to meet with or talk to their donors by phone. Too many fundraising positions are filled by people who are afraid to have an actual conversation with their supporters.

The issue in each of these scenarios is the same.

Who are your donors? Do you know?

So many of the barriers we face in fundraising come from our misunderstandings about the people who support us—our donors—and why they contribute to us and our creative pursuits. In this chapter, I will tackle some of the myths we collectively hold about donors, paint an image of who your donors are, and share ideas about ways you can connect with them.

We need to start here because it's critical to debunk some of the myths we believe about supporters. That's because they act as stumbling points in our quest to raise support for our efforts. For many of us, the mental picture of who is a donor, let alone our donor, creates our first challenge to overcome in fundraising. If from the beginning you don't know what a donor looks like, how are you going to find one?

Common Myths About Donors.

Myth #1: You Don't Know Who Your Donors Are.

Many times clients and organizations have told me that they don't know who to ask for donations. I promise: Your donors are out there. Right there in front of you, in fact. They are following you and rooting for you to succeed. Hard to believe, but they are there just waiting to be asked to help.

You can find your donors among:

»Your volunteers

»People who sign up on your mailing list

»Friends and family

»Ticket buyers

»Social media followers

The fact is, you touch more people than you think on a daily basis. The key is tuning in to your ever-growing list of connections and thinking about them as potential supporters.

Fact: Your donors are all around you already.

Myth #2: All The Donor Cares About Is A Tax Deduction.

It's crucial to take down this myth right up front. Deep down you probably don't believe that all a donor cares about is a tax deduction. We sure do use a lot of time, however, expressing that belief to our communities. Why else would we all send end-of-year solicitations? Why else remind people over and over that they can receive a tax deduction for their gift? Why do we worry so much about sending out the tax deduction letter when a gift comes in, instead of just saying "thank you"? Understand that saving money on their taxes is a very minor factor in most donors' decision making.

Here's what your donors care about:

»Your mission or vision

»Your work itself

»How donating makes them feel as a co-contributor to your vision or work

»The sense of being a part of something greater than or beyond themselves

»You

Fact: Your donor wants to play a part in your work. It helps them to feel fulfilled.

Myth #3: There Is One Major Donor Out There Who Will Cover All Your Needs With One Big Check.

Wouldn't it be great if that super-rich person in our community just wrote us a big check? Of course, it would! That's the fantasy.

While there are major donors in the world, many of them have found their causes and are already actively supporting them. That's not to say you won't someday find your major donor, but don't put all your hopes in that basket. Your major donor will come from your world, and over time they will grow in their support of you.

Very rarely do donors start their relationship with anyone they want to support with a big check. There is usually a period of feeling out the cause they want to support. If their giving meets their goals and they feel as if their donation is being put to good use, donors will be prepared to make larger and larger gifts in time. Your big donors will come from your little donors, not from your efforts to get that one big check up front. To "play the lottery," so to speak, by placing your focus on finding that one big donor is to fail in working to building a community of supporters who will give more long term than that one-time "sugar daddy."

Fact: There is a big-gift supporter out there for you. But you need to show all of your supporters how their gifts are benefitting your cause, and the big-gift supporter is far more likely to increase his or her gifts.

Myth #4: There Is Only A Finite Pool Of Donors Who Will Support Your Work/ Discipline/Field.

We can be deterred in our fundraising efforts because we believe we can only tap into the pool of donors who support work similar to the work we are doing. This is untrue.

I have witnessed, for instance, new theater companies all over the country starting off with this mindset. These companies believed they needed to get the people who support larger theater companies to support them. While there may be a crossover between the two pools of supporters, your supporters will support you because of you and your particular vision, and they will come from your world and efforts.

For example, if you are a dance company, your donors will come from the people who bought tickets to your show or the families of the dancers performing in the show.

If you are a musician, you may find your donors from past show attendees, past album buyers, or among your neighbors.

Focus on your mission and efforts, and start to identify your potential supporters.

Fact: Your constituents will be yours. Their various relationships with anyone outside your sphere does not affect you.

Myth #5: The Donor Has A Very Fragile Psyche.

This myth springs from the fear that if we ask someone for too much money (or ask at all), they will be offended. Or that if our solicitation letter is not perfect, they'll throw it in the trash. Or that if we don't hear from them, they are not interested in supporting us. Or that because they said no once, they never want to support us ever again.

None of these assumptions or any of their variations are true. They are beliefs we create in our minds and project onto donors. A client of mine recently went out on a limb to ask an old friend and supporter to make a lead gift for her upcoming campaign. After the conversation and the Ask, her friend said no to the amount. He did, however, thank her for thinking about him and encouraged her to keep on asking, even telling her when better times of the year were for him. He owned a series of restaurants, and a lot of his money was tied up in the business. Donors can handle your Ask.

Fact: Donors are not that fragile.

Myth #6: Donors Are Scary.

Maybe you're noticing that fear is one of the great barriers in fundraising, and here it raises its head again. Many of us are afraid of our donors. We are afraid they will say no. We are afraid we will overstep our bounds with them. Many of us fear to reach out to people for money.

Talking about money has become taboo. Money can be a touchy subject in our relationships. But this particular relationship, between the donor and the artist, involves the need for funds, and everyone knows it. It's not a secret that creative efforts need cash to make them real. Do not let fear of the donor hinder your ability or the need to ask for money.

Rest assured that donors are not to be feared. They are, in fact, some of the most passionate people out there, and they are very interested in us and our work. To use an old phrase, they are people who put their pants on one leg at a time, just like us.

Fact: Donors are also wonderful people who will care enough to make a gift to support you if you ask them.

Myth #7: I Have To Deceive Or Trick A Donor Into Giving.

We need to understand that donors give because they want to. Donors go through a process of thinking about their gift. Even if their giving seems to be the impulse to you, the donor made a conscious choice to give a gift to you.

Supporters give because they feel inspired. They give because their personal needs match your goals. You don't have to do anything but be honest about what you need and what you need it for. As long as you are genuine to your needs, you will find donors who want to support them. If you are dishonest about your efforts, you will not be able to keep donors. Eventually, their needs and your efforts will not match.

I have seen so many arts groups leave their true missions to chase down specific monies. For a long time, arts funding was geared toward supporting arts education in schools. Too many groups tried to create "educational" programs to get that money. The thinking was that it would help them support their main efforts. Unfortunately, these efforts almost invariably led to hard-to-manage programs and unsuccessful results in those educational programs. The money dried up, and the groups were back to square one regarding focused, legitimate fundraising.

Fact: You don't need to trick donors and bend yourself out of shape to get funds.

SO, WHO ARE DONORS?

Donors believe in your work.

Donors have almost always participated in your work in one capacity or another before they give. Donors know who you are. Many have followed your growth and are interested in where you are going next. Many times these people follow you in spite of your lack of communication with them.

Donors want to see you or your project succeed, and they want to know they helped.

That is to say, they sense and want more of a relationship with you and your work. Here's where the beauty of it lies: You are trying to accomplish something that requires money, and here comes a donor who wants to provide those funds. In you and your work, they have found a way they can help, and they're personally investing to see the idea succeed.

Donors share your vision of the world.

There are thousands of other creative people in the world, but your donors chose you. Something about what you are saying and doing resonates with them, otherwise, why would they support you?

Donors need to give.

Why do they need to? Because of how good it makes them feel. Some want to be recognized publically, while some want to remain anonymous, but all of them want that great feeling that comes when they've helped to make something happen.

Donors come from all walks of life.

Some are wealthy, and some are living paycheck to paycheck. Your donors share one thing, however: a love of you and your work.

Donors want to feel close to you.

They give because it's their way of connecting. They want to hear from you, and they want to know about your vision, your creative process. Most of all, they want to feel they are a part of your artistic journey.

Your donors are already in your world. They are. It's time to move misunderstanding and fear out of the way and let them support you.

Once you rid your mind of the myths about who donors are, you are already well down the pathway to raising the money you need.

Too many times I see fundraising fail because the messaging only focuses on your needs. I need donations because I want to do this project. I need your gift because we are going through a tough time. Donate to us because we perform this particular function in our community. Over and over again, I see solicitations that follow one of these themes.

Now you know this is one-sided.

It's essential that you start thinking now about the ways a donation can meet not only your needs but also the needs of your donor.

With that in mind, let's move ahead, and look carefully at how to apply this knowledge to the different aspects of fundraising.

Chapter 7: Cultivation

One of the core elements of fundraising is building a strong connection with your donors. In my experience with organizations and artists, it is often overlooked or undervalued.

For that reason, this chapter focuses on cultivating your relationship with current and potential supporters—or the art of relating to them when you are not asking for money.

I live outside of Washington, D.C., and have always been deeply engaged in politics. So, naturally, I started getting involved in campaigns and supporting my local politicians with donations.

On my last birthday, I received a call from a number I didn't recognize, so I let it go to voicemail. When I finally received the voicemail, I found out the call was from my Congressman wishing me a happy birthday. It was a cool message, and it was a blast sharing it with my friends. Now, I don't believe that he actually cared that it was my birthday, and I am certain that a staff member just gave him a card with my name and phone number on it (along with a handful of other people who had birthdays or other special events going on), and said: "Call him." Doesn't matter. The call made me feel recognized and appreciated, and I am more likely to make another donation to a future campaign because of the outreach.

This is a case in point as to why it's important to reach out sometimes when you don't need something.

I've already highlighted the importance of the Thank you. That one small part of the process makes a world of difference, because in one beautiful, proactive step you acknowledge the donor, make them feel important, and do it without any expecting something in return.

A lot of goodwill is generated when you turn your focus onto your donors and validate them. And that in itself is hugely important. Connecting with people when you don't need money from them is a practice you should be mindful of regularly doing. If you only talk to your supporters when you need something, you are going to make them feel as if all they are for you is a bank account.

Organizations big and small fall into the poor habit I call, "communicate only when we need something." Newsletters are begrudgingly created and sent so infrequently they come across like an afterthought.

The beautiful thing is that the solution to this deficit in communication is completely easy: Make a simple plan to reach out to people when you're not asking them for money.

All right, I get it:

»You're too busy

»You don't know what to say

»You don't want to bother people

Well, let's push past those barriers because doing so is crucial for the long haul.

First, let's consider the possibility that you are too busy. I do understand. You are underfunded, short staffed, and have your work to do. But if you want to get past being underfunded, want to hire more staff, or need the space to focus, raising more money will assist you with all of that. You get more money by building a better pool of supporters.

With this in mind, do you see how vital it is for you engage in the practice of reaching out to your donors and planning it into your schedule?

You can start this by setting up a simple process, one to which you can dedicate yourself. Certainly, whatever plan you create needs to work for you. The more comfortable and realistic the process, the more likely you will be to follow it.

Here are some examples of general ways you can reach out when not asking for money:

- Ask supporters for advice and thoughts on a topic or idea. "What do you think about me exploring this idea?"

- Express gratitude or appreciation for some connection you had with them. "It was great seeing you at x event" or "I appreciate your help with x, y, and z."

- Share with them news from your broader community. "Did you see our sister company is doing x next week?"

- Share thoughts and musings from recent travel or tour. "When I was in Italy I thought a lot about how the Italians support the arts. I wanted to share that with you."

- Send exciting photos when you have them.

- Share an interesting anecdote.

- Express to your supporters when you feel excited.

Use these types of events as triggers to reach out to your list of contacts. The next time something is interesting to you, think about if it might be interesting to others and start reaching out about it.

I'll illustrate for you the simplest process I can think of to set up a non-solicitation communication system.

Buy a bunch of index cards (any size will do), and a box for them to go into. (Honestly, a rubber band will work as well. The goal is to keep all the index cards together.) On each index card write the name, phone number, and email of one of your donors or special supporters. Put those cards in whatever order you want.

Then when something exciting happens with your work—let's say you received your first big grant—take the card on top of the stack and call or email that person with the exciting news. Keep going as far as you can go, always moving the person you just contacted to the back of the stack and moving on to the next person. Some days you will be able to get through the entire stack of names. Other days you might only be able to get through a few. It doesn't matter. What matters most is that eventually, you will touch everyone you need to touch.

There's always exciting news or developments with a project your supporters funded. You only need to let the exciting events in your world trigger an impulse to reach out to someone. People who support you want to share your excitement, and if your system is simple enough and fits well into your life, you will be able to connect with them in deeply meaningful ways that make them feel connected to you. After all, you cared enough about them to call and share the good news.

I illustrated this concept with a deck of index cards. I can't think of anything easier. You can replicate that idea, however, in whatever way makes the most sense to you. Maybe you love using a certain computer program. Perhaps there's a mobile application you like and can use for this purpose. Maybe you are equipped with the latest development and fundraising software.

What matters is that you commit to this as a regular process.

I want to encourage you here to work on being as honest and sincere as you can be with your communications. Everything I have listed can easily become carefully edited marketing or grant copy. While that can be fine, it won't resonate as powerfully with a donor as a message that is honest and comes from the heart.

In the end, it's just important that you talk to your supporters. And as with the Ask, the more intimate you can make your non-Ask conversation, the more powerful it will be. The act of talking to a donor by any means when not asking for money will move you far ahead of hundreds of other people and groups in their estimation. And making a phone call to tell them about the progress of the project to which they donated will raise you to the stratosphere regarding connection with them.

Yes, it's that easy. Even if you don't consider yourself a "people person," just pick up the phone and call the donor. Sometimes barriers are just in our heads. This leads me to the third barrier you may need to overcome: You don't want to bother people.

Guess what: You won't. If a person can't talk on the phone, they won't answer. Leave a cheerful voicemail telling them what you wanted to say and letting them know there's no need to call back unless they'd like to hear more information. Then move on to the next person. Maybe the person you called sounds super busy. Quickly get out your message and invite them to call you another time or email you if they want to learn more.

Of course, you can always send the one-on-one email. The donor will read it when they have the time and may never respond. It's all good.

Whatever you do to reach out, you will be moving ahead with the important process of showing your donors that you care about them. It may be foreign to them at first. Few people are doing this. Even fewer are doing it with any consistency. Your efforts to communicate more often and when you are not "selling" anything will make you stand out in a world crowded with people and organizations that don't. I promise, though, that your supporters will get over the foreign feeling created by your efforts and quickly come to welcome it. They will start to recognize your number and gladly take the call and chat longer and longer. They may start calling and emailing back.

I remember in one of my roles making a conscious effort to reach out regularly. The first time I would reach people and say, "Hello, I'm Damian Sinclair from x organization," I could palpably feel the unease on the other end of the line. They were bracing themselves for what had to be an Ask. When I expressed what I needed to and wished them a beautiful night, I could tell they were surprised and relieved. The more I did it, the warmer the conversations became.

The point is that you and your donor will be more and more engaged in good communication. And a more engaged donor is going to give and support more often and is very likely to give.

Chapter 8: The Power of Networking

It is often said that people give to people, not to organizations. While that's not entirely accurate—some people give because they believe passionately in the organization—this axiom is still good advice. Even if your organization addresses an urgent need in the community and utilizes, every dollar raised with maximum efficiency, if donors don't like you or don't know you, they likely won't give.

Coffee Meetings

To increase your network, and ultimately the fundraising dollars, it's recommended that you set a benchmark for coffee meetings, such as meeting one person per week. Coffee meetings are an informal and inexpensive way for you to learn about people, for them to learn about you and your organization, and to ultimately build a network.

You must remember two things at these meetings. First, do not solicit them for money right off the bat. This is likely your first meeting and soliciting may feel unnatural. Second, be authentic, honest, and interested in the conversation. Do not treat the meeting as another way to increase your business card volume. Instead, treat this person like a friend—someone who has taken the time to meet with you. Treating people with respect increases the respect that they will have for you.

Who should you meet with? Anyone and everyone. As a beginner fundraiser, do not discriminate. Think about making connections with people you have met in the past. Make connections with new people. Because the costs of both time and money are low, meeting with people you may never talk to again is not a huge loss. Also, you should never underestimate what you can learn from people and how you can help them. These meetings shouldn't just be about ways to help you exclusively.

Finding people to meet with can be as simple as asking colleagues or doing quick Internet research. Communities are diverse, and if you are genuinely trying to learn more, meeting people will be easy and rewarding. As you become more experienced and your network grows, you can decrease the frequency of these meetings, and become more selective about who you meet with.

There are two final points to keep in mind. First, ask for recommendations after each meeting. Once others learn about you, they will have ideas and suggestions for how to help and who else you should be talking to. Secondly, follow up with the people you meet. While a more formal approach is to send a thank you note, send a quick e-mail instead. Reference something you talked about or follow through on offer to show them around your organization. Whatever you decide to write is up to you, but make sure you follow up and are grateful.

Networking Events
In addition to coffee meetings, another way to meet people and build your network is to attend events. Personally, I prefer one-on-one meetings rather than larger, more structured networking events. While you can still meet people, these event encounters tend to be less personal. Most attendees quickly grab business cards, which seems disingenuous, since most won't contact you. If you are more of an extrovert and don't mind the network "freeloaders," then you may want to attend a few networking events.

Business Awards Luncheons
Luncheons are similar to networking events. Most likely, your community's business news outlet hosts business awards luncheons. Awards luncheons might focus on business leaders or fast-growing companies. These are excellent ways to meet new prospects for your organization. Sitting at a random table allows for an opportunity to meet new people and learn about their respective business. Additionally, you learn facts about your community and the business environment, which is helpful knowledge for your role.

Join A Few Clubs
It is important to balance your time between the organization you are employed by and joining civic organizations. But these organizations—while rewarding in their right—can lead to connections, and ultimately more support for your organization. Many towns and cities have civic or volunteer organizations, such as Rotary, and you should consider joining one.

Information Is Power

Consult other experienced fundraising professionals in the area. If you are new to fundraising or the area, consider reaching out to counterparts. Other fundraisers may be good resources for learning about the community—both the opportunities and the challenges. Offer to buy them coffee and have a one-hour chat. Most counterparts would welcome the chance to help you. You will be astonished what you can learn from an hour long conversation!

Read Local And Regional News

It's probably good advice for anyone in any profession, but it's worth reiterating: read! Reading local news and consuming information about your specific industry helps you grow as a person and as a professional. It allows you to become a more engaged citizen, one who is aware of current issues and trends. Also, you may be able to connect your profession—in this case, fundraising—to the local economy, news, and events. Reading the local newspaper and having a broad base of knowledge provides you with another tool when you encounter new people.

Three Main Sources Of Unearned Revenue

As you probably know, a company's revenue comes in a variety of ways. In the nonprofit realm, this is also true. Funding for nonprofits can be split into earned revenue and unearned revenue. Earned revenue is money earned from your organization by engaging directly in its mission. For instance, a film society might sell tickets to their screenings. This money is considered earned revenue because the sales related to its mission.

On the other hand, unearned revenue is money that is made through fundraising. There are three main types of unearned revenue: grants, individual giving, and business giving.

Grants

One of the three main sources of funding for nonprofit organizations is grants. Grants typically come from foundations or local, regional, or national organizations that specialize in something, for example, an arts council. Granting organizations exist solely to distribute money in the form of grants.

Finding Grants

Even though granting organizations grant money, acquiring the money involves careful investigation. Many reliable sources exist for researching and finding granting institutions. One resource is your local library. Many libraries have non-profit sections containing books and digital material that can easily narrow your search to find funding for your specific organization. Often, you can limit your search to granting organizations based on geographic region, the mission of the organization, and frequency of funding. In addition to your local library, consider online searches as a quick and effective way to uncover local, regional, and national funding organizations. Most likely, there are many foundations in a nearby city that you have never heard of.

Getting Acquainted with Foundations or Granting Organization

Before you apply for a grant from a funding organization, do your research. It is important to evaluate the granting organization's mission, website, and historical funding commitments. Often, you can glean information about funding priorities through their website. For example, if you're looking into a foundation that supports the arts, does the organization tend to grant more dance-oriented funding? If so, then it is possible the organization has a special affinity—not necessarily specified or outlined—for dance. Keep in mind, though, that past funding history is no guarantee of future funding decisions. But it can give insight into what the organization tends to find attractive. Most funding organizations publish their mission and past funding either on their website or in press releases. A quick web search should yield good results.

Know the People Making the Decisions

If it has been said once, it has been said thousands of times: fundraising is about relationships. It is no different when you are applying for organizational funds. In addition to knowing the organization's mission and past funding decisions, it is just as critical to get to know the influential people in the organization. Building these relationships will be critical to your success. Attempt to remove the "fourth wall" between your organization and the funding organization. (By "fourth wall", I mean the rigid, transactional dynamic present before a relationship has evolved).

Place yourself in their shoes. They would probably prefer to give to an organization of people with whom they are familiar as opposed to giving a "blind" grant to an organization they know little about.

How can you get to know them? One possibility is by inviting them to a tour of your facility. A tour can be extremely eye opening and will reinforce the needs of your organization.

Another idea to consider is hosting a cocktail party. (You could even combine the two and host the cocktail party at your facility). Cocktail parties are excellent social avenues for getting to know funding organizations and their administrators. Make sure you have current board members and strong ambassadors attend these events. This ensures you have trusted leaders praising your organization.

A third effective way to build relationships is to have an informal hour-long coffee chat. Coffee chats are one of the simplest ways for you to learn about someone. In return, they get to learn about you. Bring organizational materials to the meeting, but don't make it a sales pitch. You are there to learn about the other person (What are their likes and dislikes? What makes them passionate?). Each of these encounters only goes to strengthen your ultimate proposal to their organization.

When employed, any of these methods can be effective ways to build relationships with potential funding organizations. Consider them before applying.

Follow Directions

One of the easiest steps in applying for a grant is simply following the directions. Many applicants neglect certain rules that the granting organization requires. Don't make this mistake. Funding organizations receive many requests. If they can find ways to eliminate your application, and thus the volume of grant proposals, they will. So if the application asks for a submission to be paper clipped, don't staple it. If the organization asks that you limit your application to three pages, don't submit four. And, if you have any questions, ask! Staff members are often available to assist your organization in presenting the best possible application.

Follow Up with Foundation Requests and Proposals

After a proposal is submitted, your job is not complete. Unless the funding organization specifically asks that no follow-ups occur after a submitted proposal, make it a goal to follow up within a week after the proposal is submitted. This ensures that the organization received your application, and it demonstrates your commitment.

Individual Fundraising
Why do individuals give? Much could be written on the subject of why individuals give to an organization. Donors are inspired to give for a myriad of reasons, and it would be an unnecessary exercise to examine all of them. This discussion will explore how a fundraiser can discover or influence how a prospective donor might give.

First, consider what you know or can learn about this individual. Passion often drives funding decisions for individuals. So what are they passionate about? For instance, an SVP of a local bank may have minored in film. If your organization screens films, learning this can yield results. While exploring what makes a donor excited, you may find interests that coincide with your organization's mission. Your goal is to align those interests with your mission.

The second approach to individual fundraising is to learn about a prospective donor's influencers. Perhaps one of your board members is friends with or is related to this prospect. Approach the friend and seek their advice. A friend may be inclined to help you ask, suggest an ask amount, or provide insight into the donor. Seeking additional information is always recommended before approaching a new donor.

As mentioned earlier, individual giving is complex and varied. Much of your success will depend on a donor's passion, your organization's mission, and, as always, relationships. Consider each of these as you venture into individual giving.

Always Check for Matching Dollars

Your organization can double the impact of an individual's contribution by receiving a matching gift. It's common practice for a donor's employer to match gifts, especially at larger companies. Consider implementing an option for listing employment on a pledge form—whether your form is written or electronic. This way you can not only track where donors work, but you can also research a company's matching gift policy. (This is usually located on a company's website).

Annual Campaigns

An annual campaign is one tool nonprofits can use to generate income. This model is probably the most widely used and recognized. Typically, solicitation letters signed by your executive director are sent on an annual basis. The letters outline your organization's benefits to the community and why you are soliciting funds. The benefit to this strategy is that you can purchase mailing lists from a variety of sources to target your solicitation. Also, your annual appeal is regular communication with potential donors who you may not otherwise engage with.

Although this strategy is ubiquitous, it counters most of the logic and advice in this book. Annual appeals typically fail to leverage relationships since they are usually sent blindly. Without relationships, raising money is difficult. I am not recommending preceding this path, as it does yield results. But, after those donors are "in," you should work to deepen that relationship, so they become return supporters.

Chapter 9: Important Fundraising Tools

Timing

After a certain time on the job as a fundraiser, your supervisors will begin to expect results. They will expect success in raising money for the organization. Of course, they are right; you should be bringing in money. But, remember that fundraising takes time and requires a plan. While some fundraising skills may be easily transferred between organizations and quickly implemented, some strategies take time to implement and patience to see through.

Perhaps you are new to your community. If so, you will need to begin meeting people. Connecting with people might be your first goal as you begin your new role. Remember, people give to people and not necessarily just to the organization. So you will need to build a network of individuals. Expecting to build a reliable and rich network in a few months will not be easy. A year of meeting people and learning your community is ideal.

Fundraising takes a plan. To assuage any concerns about your ability to perform well in your job, you need a good plan. You need to know what tools you have available to you as a fundraiser, and you need to map out a strategy. Project out to a year from your current situation, and work backward. If you have a fundraising goal of X, break the goal into manageable slices or quarters (three months). Don't become overwhelmed by the ultimate goal; it's a journey, not a sprint.

Be A Connector, Not An Asker

One of the major hurdles for many beginner fundraisers is the anxiety of asking for money. However, a slight perspective change can alleviate this. Instead of thinking that you need the savviest sales pitch for your organization, consider yourself as a connector. Your job is to link your organization's mission and a prospective donor's passion.

Prospective donors are human. And all humans have passions. When you meet new people, you should try to learn about their passions. What makes them excited? You may discover they are passionate about education. So your job would be to spotlight how your organization's education programs would be satisfying to them.

Rather than being an aggressive salesperson, your role shifts to connecting the dots between a human with deep interests and what your organization produces. That's something to be proud of, and should not be an anxiety-producing task.

If you approach prospective donor meetings with the intent of "closing the deal," your anxiety will be high, and you will likely be unsuccessful. But if you approach each new meeting as the beginning of a relationship, your anxiety will decrease, your satisfaction will rise, and you ultimately will raise more money.

Partnership And Two-Way Giving
In fundraising, you should always approach conversations with prospective and current donors with a relationship mindset. Everyone can spot a fake and will know when you are only looking out for yourself by getting them to write a check. While your job could be boiled down to transactional check-writing, it is highly recommended that you not miss the forest for the trees. Appreciate the relationship you will build with donors. Not only will this result in more long-term support for your organization, but it will also allow you to build relationships with fascinating people in your community. You'll realize fundraising is richer than strictly money exchanging hands.

Workplace Campaigns
One strategy for nonprofit fundraising is workplace campaigns. Workplace campaigns are run inside a company that is typically also a business supporter. They ask individual employees to contribute to your organization. To make the process even more efficient, companies may offer payroll deduction for their employees. Typically campaigns are run for a day or a week inside the company. Incentives such as "wear jeans to work day" and pizza parties are hosted to encourage giving. Consider creative methods of illustrating your organization's mission, for example, having performers at the company during lunch hour or some similar entertainment.

Obviously, to make these campaigns successful, you need a key member of the staff to be a "cheerleader" or ambassador for your organization. Ideally, this would be the CEO or owner.

Compelling Reasons To Give

Never underestimate the power of emotion when it comes to fundraising. Your ability to convey a compelling story about why your organization exists and why it should be supported are tools in your arsenal.

Whatever marketing materials your organization utilizes, the message should be compelling and emotional. You should seek to convey why your organization exists and less about what you do. The narrative of why your organization exists becomes the foundational building block as you talk to donors—both business and individual.

Where Does the Money Go?

One compelling strategy is to create a more "real" experience for a prospective donor. If a prospective donor understands how their support assists an organization—as opposed to assuming it goes into a big pot of money—they will be more inclined to give. This information can be in your head, at the ready for meetings, or written on a postcard you email to prospective donors.

Your Website And Social Media

With the increased fame of the Internet and its many components, much could be written on the subject of Internet fundraising. Because the subject is still new and successful strategies have not been tested over a long period, I will not devote too much space to this subject. The recommendation from this book is to focus on your organization's website before you delve into auxiliary marketing strategies. After all, if you send out a tweet aren't you ultimately driving folks back to your website? And if that website is in poor condition, it doesn't matter how clever your tweet is.

Focus your organization's energy on creating a content-rich but easy-to-use website. Websites that lack information—especially current information—are not worthwhile. Ensure users have a reason to visit your website and to visit often. Also, it is critical to have a very simple method of giving online. The more cumbersome the donation process, the more frustrated your donors will become, and the fewer donations you will receive. The donation button should be identifiable but not invasive. Once it is clicked, the landing page should be clean and concise. Some organizations do this very well, while others present a dreary face to the public.

It should be noted that websites are your organization's public face. Do not underestimate the significance that consumers, patrons, and users of your site place on it. They, whether consciously or not, will judge the professionalism of your organization based on outdated content, passé style, or clumsy navigation. If your organization has a website, then make sure it represents your organization just like any other marketing materials. Donors and patrons can make engagement decisions based solely on an organization's website. Make sure your organization's site is above average.

Social media can often be a distraction to a resource-strapped non-profit. That said, it can still be an effective method of marketing, especially for a younger audience. Just be sure your social media engagement isn't a burden and has a thoughtful strategy underlying it. Many times nonprofits rush to the next social media fad adding it to their ever-growing list. Just because the tool exists, doesn't necessarily mean it's ideal for your overall marketing strategy. Be thoughtful in what social media you utilize and constantly ask yourself how it enables your organization to fulfill its mission.

Fundraising Pyramid

In the early stages, you may utilize many planning tools to help you achieve your goals. One of those tools should be a fundraising pyramid. For instance, perhaps your fundraising goal is $100,000. Initially, that number may seem daunting as you slip into your first week as a fundraiser. You might ask yourself, who or what company would ever give at that level and where would I ever begin to raise that high of an amount? This fundraising tool can assuage some of your anxiety.

A fundraising pyramid is simple: it segments a larger goal into smaller chunks, making the overall goal more manageable and practical. Most likely, a single $100,000 gift is unrealistic. It's more realistic to have smaller goals that eventually total your overall goal. Based on data from past fundraising, you may know that a $25,000 gift could be possible from one of your higher-capacity donors. But more than one $25,000 gift is unlikely. Also, you could probably surmise that receiving ten $1,000 gifts is much easier than ten $5,000 gifts, and so on. Based on common sense and a little research, you build mini-goals inside of your larger goal, making the execution of raising these funds more realistic and practical.

Annual Report

If there is one marketing and fundraising piece you should give considerable time to, it is the annual report. Annual reports are excellent development tools for your organization. Do not underestimate the powerful story that your annual report tells donors and the public. It is recommended that annual reports be mailed to donors of a certain level and above. These reports share the progress of your organization over the past year, highlighting your financial standing and the programs you made possible.

Annual reports should contain many visual images, be colorful, and tell a positive story of your organization. When mailed, annual reports typically include a letter from the executive director—another vehicle to tell your organization's story and how you worked to achieve the mission of the organization. An annual report is a good tool to have in your back pocket as you meet with prospects. Donors who are savvy will look to an organization's annual report as an indicator of whether their financial investment is worth making.

Explore Governmental Funding

At some point, your organization should consider the city, county, and federal funding. Each one of these carries its trials and rewards. Once you have mastered the strategies in this book and had a year or two of experience, I would recommend exploring these additional fundraising streams—if your organization has not already done so.

Checklist For The Beginner Fundraiser

Learn about the community you are in—whether you are new to the community or not. This includes reading local publications and attending events.

Meet one-on-one with people in your community or network! Be authentic, meet a variety of people, and learn from them. Ask questions. At the end of each meeting, ask who else you should meet.

Begin meeting with prospective donors and utilize your fundraising tools when meeting with them. Are they interested in your mission? Are they interested in pure philanthropy, visibility for their organization, associate or client engagement, or a combination of all these things?

Involve volunteers and boards with your fundraising. Use volunteers to steward new donors, make solicitations, and send notes of gratitude.

Always be ready to learn and always be open to new opportunities because you never know where a supporter might be.

Chapter 10: Motivation To Give

Most fundraisers will have attended fundraising seminars where there is at least one major presentation on 'What Motivates a Benefactor to Give to a Cause or Project.' We are reminded that the major motivations for people to give benefactions are to be sought after and to feel like a worthwhile member of a worthwhile group. According to many experienced fundraisers, these two motivators are key universal aspirations.

There are many other motivations, and it's important to know and understand them.

Motivations for Giving
- Need for self-esteem: Some people build their self-esteem and self-image through giving.
- Need for recognition from others: Giving helps them to build their social status or prestige in the eyes of others. They wish to be recognized publicly for their good deeds.
- Pride of association: People give to be associated with a particular organization, its programs, and its personnel. Special communications and ceremonies can nurture pride.
- The sense of community responsibility and love of the Arts: People may give because they believe strongly in the value of the Arts and feel morally accountable for supporting them. Even people who rarely or never attend the ballet or symphony concerts believe in the importance of these Art forms to the community and therefore help to support them.
- Good business: Many business owners gain image-building benefits and visibility by supporting worthwhile organizations.
- Forced giving: Some people are pressured by managers to give at their place of work.
- Family tradition: Some people give to organizations because their parents did.
- Desire for immortality or in memory of a family member or loved one: Many benefactors give so that their name or the

names of their family members, friends or pets will be remembered long after they are dead.

- Guilt: People give to alleviate feelings of guilt from their past.

However, international success coach, Anthony Robbins firmly believes that two basic and powerful underlying motivators affect all human beings –inspiration and desperation.

The Motivation Direction Programme

In NLP terms, these key elements of motivation are known as the 'Motivation Direction Programme.' People are either motivated by the thought of obtaining something pleasurable as a result of what they are doing or are about to do (motivated towards pleasure) or they are motivated by the thought of escaping from something uncomfortable (motivated away from pain).

Brian Tracey describes the two motivation categories as "desire for gain" and the "fear of loss," which are both useful for different situations. NLP research has indicated that people, on the whole, adopt either one or the other for all situations.

For example, if a person uses the 'towards pleasure' motivation, he or she will be motivated by goals and the promise of rewards. These motivated towards pleasure people will arrange a holiday because they want to experience enjoyment; they will change their occupation to achieve a higher salary and status; and will choose friends who challenge and stimulate them.

People who are motivated by moving away from pain will arrange a holiday to escape their stressful environment. They will change jobs because the present one has become unbearable. They will choose friends who are undemanding.

In a solicitation situation, it is essential to include both motivational strategies, starting firstly with the obstacles that your organization is overcoming by implementing the project for which you are seeking a benefaction. This is the away from pain strategy. It is also crucial to mention some of the problems that might be encountered when the project is established and how your organization plans to overcome them. Then introduce all the exciting, innovative benefits of the project and the details of what and who will benefit from it. This is the towards pleasure strategy.

This means that you have satisfied the 'away from' motivated person by pointing out the problems and how you will move 'away' from these, and you have satisfied the 'towards person' by listing the solutions and the benefits of the exciting project that your organization is planning with their assistance.

Many politicians use this technique in their speeches, first introducing a problem then following it with a solution. Leaving the solution to the last part of the speech means the listener is left with a positive impression of the speaker however bad the problems may appear to be.

Similarities And Differences

As fundraisers, we must be aware of how potential benefactors consider the information being given to them. Some people look firstly for similarities, familiarity and sameness in a proposal before looking at differences and variety. Others seek things that are different and new before they consider what is similar and familiar.

It is interesting to see how advertisers include these two separate groups in major advertising campaigns. For example, advertisements for the latest model cars draw attention to 'this new improved model with the qualities you have come to expect together with the very latest technological innovations.' What an extremely clever way of including both the similarities and differences.

Broad Picture Or Detail?

Another difference between people that we need to be aware of is that some like to be given a general overall global picture of a project while others demand the details. How can you recognize which type of person you're dealing with?

It wasn't difficult to recognize a 'broad picture person' who would not welcome me going into a detailed description of the project.

Another potential benefactor for the same project asked:

"What sorts of people come to the Agency for treatment? What state are they in when they arrive? How will the expansion impact on the standards of treatment? Do they all receive the same treatment program? Do you have various categories depending on the drug they are addicted to?"

This particular solicitation took place over a two-hour period with the potential benefactor asking for information on every facet of the organization's work.

Never begin a description of the project until you are certain which category your benefactor falls into. A 'big picture' person will become irritated and bored with detail and the 'detail person' will think your organization hasn't put enough thought into the project if he or she isn't given the full and detailed facts.

Potential major gift benefactors are 'broad picture' people, but it is worth the effort to wait and listen before proceeding.

Matchers And Mismatchers

Lurking amongst potential benefactors are the people termed 'Mismatchers.' They are the people who, within the first five minutes of meeting you, ask "What is new or different about your organization?" These are the people who love change and variety and will be keen to assist programs within your organization that will bring about rapid change to people or events.

There are also people known as the 'Matchers' who like to help organizations that have been in the marketplace since their grandparent's time or before. They like people, situations, and events to stay the same. These people will give to organizations or programs that are familiar.

Places, People, Things, Information and Actions

I'm sure you would agree that most people have specific interests in life. Underlying these interests are five general categories of interest - places, people, things, information and actions - things of which a person may predominantly favor (filter) just one. Knowing which is their predominant category is extremely valuable regarding gift solicitation.

People Who Favour Places

People who favor places are very easy to identify. When they choose a job, the location of the company will be a major motivating factor. They will often move from where they were brought up if it isn't a pleasant environment as the location is more important to them than being close to family or friends. These people are acutely aware of their environment and would be most unhappy meeting in shabby surroundings despite the worthiness of the organization. It is vital that these people are offered a solicitation meeting in luxurious offices, a top class hotel or club or a tastefully decorated private home. These are the people who are interested in giving to environmental issues; enhancement of the landscape and refurbishment of neglected buildings such as concert halls and listed buildings.

People Who Favour Things

People who favor things are mostly interested in material objects like buildings or machinery. These are the people I would approach to support a capital campaign for a new hospital wing, concert hall, lifeboat or for the computerization of a disadvantaged school.

People Who Favour People

People who favor people are interested in both individuals and group activities. They are usually found in the service and caring industries and are usually very adept at creating strong rapport. These are the people I approach to support charities that are working to improve the lives and conditions of disadvantaged children and adults (for example, Save the Children, Foundation for the Blind, and The Salvation Army).

People Who Favour Information

People who favor information are interested in academic research, the Internet, and educational institutions. This group also includes the new computer millionaires. I have found that this category of people will support the purchase of rare books, the upkeep of ancient artifacts and the development of the Internet as well as educational projects such as sponsorship of Fellowships, and provision of student bursaries.

People Who Favour Activities

People who favor activities are not so interested in why something is being done or what is happening, but more about how it is done. You can usually identify people from this group because they lead action-packed lives and tend to choose activities and even holidays that fulfill their desire for adventure and actions, e.g., white-water rafting, tennis, skiing and bicycling. These people will support organizations like Raleigh International, The Princes Trust and Mini Olympics for the disabled, or appeals for school playing fields, building gymnasiums, and swimming pools.

Proactive or Reactive?

Another useful category for a fundraiser to know is whether a person is proactive or reactive, particularly in a solicitation process.

The Proactive Person

The proactive person as a potential benefactor or volunteer is a "doer" with a strong sense of purpose. They will only become involved in an activity or project that has a result, and that is measurable and worthwhile. These people become irritable if a discussion is long-winded and verbose. They expect a clear, lucid picture of the project that needs funding. They are easy people to spot as they invariably begin a discussion with phrases such as "Let's begin now" or "Let's action this project." They will ask very direct questions and expect immediate answers. They will usually make up their minds instantly as to whether they believe a project is worth financially supporting. They also make wonderful Campaign leaders. The Campaign targets are established, and outcomes agreed, meetings finish on time, and 'sufferers of verbal diarrhea' are cured in an instant with a few choice words.

The Reactive Person

The reactive person, on the other hand, can be recognized by such phrases as "I think we should delay progress on this project until we've had time to consider all the ramifications" or "Let me think about that for a while longer." These individuals find it hard to take action or make a commitment and will more often block change taking place within the organization they are involved in. They are not good at planning or chairing meetings. Their strength lies in 'firefighting' or reacting to situations that may suddenly arise, and indicate the flaws in the course of action.

Again it is important to stress that people cannot be rigidly categorized as 'a proactive' or 'reactive person.' It is merely a pattern of behavior that can be recognized and dealt with accordingly.

In other words, the more we can recognize different patterns of communication the more easily we can adapt our own communication patterns to achieve the outcomes we desire.

Chapter 11: Who Should Fundraise?

Everyone within an organization is a potential fundraiser. If you are the fundraiser, you should try to ensure that everyone supports your fundraising activities. Fundraisers should make sure that they have a real understanding of the organizations' cause. Anyone with the right skills can carry out the fundraising activity, and while it can be linked to a single person, it is a whole team or organization activity.

What Skills Should A Fundraiser Have?

One of the key skills of the fundraiser is communication. Telling donors and potential supporters about the work of the organization and encouraging them to give is fundamental to fundraising. A good fundraiser will show donors and supporters how their gift will enable the organization to meet the needs of the beneficiary making a positive change.

In many smaller not-for-profits and charities, the lines between fundraiser and service provider can be blurred – often being the same person. In such cases, this person has their opportunity to enhance not only the organization's income stream but also its brand and reputation.

In some organizations, a member of staff will be designated the task of fundraising, in other cases, it might be a volunteer or committee member.

There are other options such as using a consultant, a freelance fundraiser, an outside agency or supplier. The choice is dependent on the resources of the organization.

Essentially, a good fundraiser should have the following:

- Excellent communication skills, written and verbally with different audiences;
- Planning and organizational abilities;
- Empathy with the cause;
- Understanding of finance and budgeting;
- Creativity;

-      Tack, diplomacy and good judgment.

Fundraising is not a quick way to bring in income, and anyone appointed to the task will need time and commitment from the whole organization. Raising fundraising income takes time, and it is unrealistic to expect a fundraiser to save an organization from financial disaster immediately.

Fundraising cannot be attempted at the time that a specific activity is in need of funding. Fundraising takes time – this cannot be underestimated. Relationships need to be developed, ensuring that donors feel that they know the organization, funding applications may need to be submitted which have a timeline of their own for approval. The list is endless. Planning is key and can ultimately overcome each of these barriers.

Does your charity have a business or strategic plan? – If not, then you must have one before you start. Whether you are the one to put it together or your trustees and staff, it is an important document that you will refer to time and time again during your fundraising journey. You need to know what you are fundraising for and what the long-term funding plans are. As well as this, you also need to know what type of income is needed. For example, does the organization need funds to support a project or staffing costs? Some donors will only fund projects, whereas others will provide funds to support staff and overheads.

What is your organization's experience of fundraising? Consider the following, as they will help to identify areas where fundraising can prove to be most effective:

-      Do you have a database of contacts or members that might be potential donors?
-      Has your organization been successful in past fundraising activities?
-      Who might be potential donors?
-      Could trustees, or the Board help with fundraising activities?
-      Could a partnership or a joint project with another charity or not for profit work?
-      How much money is available to invest in fundraising?

- What types of funds are needed? Do you need funds for the major project (capital) or regular day to day activities (revenue)?
- Do you have a fundraising strategy?

Types of Fundraising

There are several different types of fundraising, each fitting within each of the categories below:

- Fundraising from individuals;
- Fundraising from businesses;
- Fundraising from trusts, foundations and statutory sources;
- Fundraising from communities.

Fundraising From Individuals

Despite the recession, according to the Center on Philanthropy at Indiana University, Individuals in the USA gave $217 billion in 2011, compared with $209 billion in 2010. In the UK, the Charities Aid Foundation survey found that the public donated over £9.3 billion in 2011.

This giving can be in several different ways from giving their spare change in envelopes to collecting cash in the streets. Fundraising organizations use a mix of fundraising activities to attract and retain donors (and the point is to retain them). Income from one-off donations can be just as worthwhile as income from regular givers and the mix helps with cash flow.

The benefit of money from individual donors is that it is often 'unrestricted.' This means that it can be used for any charitable purpose the organization wishes, unlike funds from a trust or foundation, which usually has to be applied to specific projects.

When trying to attract funding from individual donors, think creatively about how to inform donors about the work your organization is doing and encourage them to give. We often develop what's called an 'appeal,' which is based on an urgent need or significant anniversary.

It is also important to keep a list of donors, whether they have given once or give regularly. It can be helpful to analyze their giving habits for future fundraising activities. For example, do they like to give at Christmas or do they prefer to support particular projects or the purchase of equipment? This information is vital and can guide you with your future fundraising activity.

How to ask individual donors for a donation?

There are many different ways. The key thing is to ask and keep on asking. Keep telling your donors about your beneficiaries and the difference their support can make to their lives. Also, don't forget to thank donors for their donation and if possible be available to answer questions from donors.

Here is a list of ways that you can engage donors and communicate to them your need for donations:

- direct mail
- Telephone calls
- Radio and television
- SMS and text messaging
- Press and media
- Internet and email

You can also collect money from passers-by or by knocking on doors. This is a good way to raise the profile of your organization and establish a relationship with your community. Collection tins are another good way of gaining individual donations. These can be left in local shops (with permission), and individuals will insert their loose change.

It is wise to set an amount that you plan to raise and don't be too greedy. You can always ask for larger amounts as your donors get to know you. Another suggestion is to break the larger amount into smaller units: 'four donations of $25 would enable us to take the inner city young people to the beach.'

Committed giving

This is the ultimate goal of your organization. This type of giving provides a regular, stable income from individuals as it allows organizations to plan for the future while continuing their day to day activities.

Donors will give regular amounts to a charity or not-for-profit often via direct debits or standing orders.

Legacy giving

This is a popular way of leaving money to a cause. Gifts are normally left in wills, and many organizations have built up huge reserves from legacy giving.

Fundraising From Business
Businesses are keen to promote their local community. Often for larger companies, their Corporate Social Responsibility (CSR) comes into play. This is where businesses consider their social, environmental and other responsibilities on the communities where their businesses are based and provide funding to give back as well as support the local community.

Payroll giving is often promoted by companies so that their employees can contribute directly from their salary. For employees, this is an easy, tax-effective way to give and it costs them less to give more. For employers, it's a great way to demonstrate a commitment to the causes that their employees care about.

Don't forget that if your corporate supporter does not have payroll giving as part of their activities, you can always introduce it to them.

Sponsorship involves businesses providing money or gifts to support a fundraising appeal. A business may be willing to sponsor an event, newsletter, banner or other activity.

Another way for businesses to be involved in fundraising is for them to give some of the profits of any product or service they are selling to charity or a not-for-profit.

Fundraising From Trusts, Foundations And Statutory Sources
There are tens of thousands of trusts and foundations in the UK and USA, not to mention the rest of the world. For many smaller organizations, grants from trusts and foundations can be a significant part of their income.

Trusts and foundations give grants to organizations that have projects or activities that match the trusts funding objectives. Some trusts are limited so can only give grants to organizations supporting specific groups like women and children. Trusts and foundations are normally charities themselves, but they may also be a Government body. These Government bodies that give funding are known as statutory funders.

Thrusts and foundations support organizations in a variety of ways. They could offer project funding over many years; capital funding towards a building or equipment or funding for you to pilot a project. Usually a charity or not-for-profit applies to the foundation or trust by filling in an application form, detailing the project or activities that they would like to conduct. Funders consider applications against their criteria and will award funds to the organization whose funding application best matches the funding criteria.

Most funders of this type will expect to see a copy of your most recent annual report and accounts. Be sure to send them what they need, but not too much information. Remember that this is competitive funding as only a certain number of projects can be funded.

Once again, if the application is successful, remember to thank the funder and keep them up to date with developments.

Fundraising from Communities
Events are popular for raising funds from communities. Whether it's a sponsored run, garden party or dinner and dance, they do require planning and the input of a committed team and can be very rewarding. The key is to promote the event and ask locally for funding to support it. Or funding can be obtained during the event itself.

Keep costs low when undertaking an event. Successful fundraising involves finding ways to reduce the cost of the fundraising activity. Think creatively.

Chapter 12: The Benefits Of Fundraising

1. Raises Awareness

As mentioned previously, fundraising is usually done by non-profit organizations for a good cause. Now, how do you think anyone can help if they do not understand what is going on and why one needs their aid?

It is not as if you can simply walk up to a person or send them an e-mail asking for money without giving them a good reason to shell out their dough. A fund-raising event opens the eyes of the possible donors by explaining and showing them what it is that they can do to help.

Some people end up giving more than they intend to once they understand where their hard-earned cash will go.

2. Survival

Unlike for-profit organizations, non-profits may not have a consistent stream of revenue or may run out of money at some point. Effectively fundraising on a continuous basis will keep the non-profit alive.

Through the aid of money raised from the fundraiser, the survival of the organization is assured.

3. Sustainability

Fundraising helps raise awareness, however, understand that this is not the only thing being raised. Due to awareness, more and more people who want to help may also come to your door and help you out in sustaining your non-profit organization.

These type of organizations can build a group of very reliable donors who aren't only willing to support their cause directly but make sure that the organization itself will last long enough to serve its function and be able to help in other capacities.

4. Creates A Network Of Givers

Fundraising functions are a great way to bring like-minded individuals together so that they can create a network that supports your cause.

Through fundraising events, a person who wanted to help can feel more comfortable by connecting with others who want to give.

5. It is A Win-Win Situation

What can one say about this? Fundraising simply makes the world a better place. Yes, it is what you can call a win-win situation.

While the guests already know that you need to cough up an amount for this fundraiser, it does not exactly mean that they are at a loss.

Yes, the overall amount of their money may decrease a little after joining a fundraiser, but it also gives them the opportunity to help in a way where they are sure their money is in good hands and will be used properly for a good cause.

You see, this is the kind of help that is a different than just directly giving the money to the person in need whom you just found on the street. Yes, one can always give fish to those in need, but it is a different and better story to teach them how to fish.

The Pillars of Fundraising

Pillars of fundraising? What are they? Well, they are sources of income that you can use in fundraising to ensure that your organization is sustainable.

You simply cannot rely on two types of income sources and just keep interchanging them. That won't do. Your non-profit organization needs to thrive and survive, so let me give you a list of these seven pillars.

1. Community-Business Partnership or Sponsorship

Sponsorship is when you connect with a business entity and make them a donor as well. This is very beneficial to the business, the non-profit organization, and the community as well. This is due to the capability of the business entity to provide for, in cash or kind, in an easier manner as compared to asking a certain individual for help.

2. Crowdfunding

It all happens online. Crowdfunding is utilized whenever funds are needed for a certain project. This method can gather a good amount of funds, just be creative enough to express your thoughts and intentions well to the Internet.

3. Donations

This method would be your classic view of fundraising. Most small non-profit organizations are afraid to ask for donations, but you should not be, even if you are mere starters. What matters is your intention, and if your sincerity shines through, there would always be people willing to help and give.

4. Grants

Grants are money that is provided by the local state, corporate trusts, the federal government, foundations, and philanthropists every year. It can be any amount. Usually billions of dollars and people and organizations who are qualified can apply to have a share of it. However, not everyone who applies for grants get approved, and the process can sometimes be long and arduous.

5. Membership or Alumni

Membership or alumni programs can provide you some renewable and predictable funds for your non-profit organization. You can have their support as long as the people from your membership or alumni programs feel that sense of belonging to you.

6. Sales

This is what we call the earned income, and you can sell just about anything, as long as they are safe and clean just like home-baked cookies or pastries. The kind of money you will earn from sales is untied money, meaning after someone pays for the merchandise or product you are selling, that's if they are not expecting any update coming from you.

7. Special Events

Many non-profit organizations do this, and so, this has become their lifeblood. You can make it fun and memorable for the donors. Below are some examples of special events that organizations host.

- Art shows
- Balls or dance night
- Festivals
- Game night
- Sponsored record attempts
- Talent contests
- Trivia nights
- Auctions

Planning Your Fundraiser

Fundraisers, while sometimes extravagant and sometimes simple, are usually fun--especially if you are the guest. Being one of those who plans it is a different story. Yes, it is still fun, but can be stressful and challenging. You have to plan it out very well to make sure that it will be unforgettable, enjoyable, and of course, can still raise the funds that you need for your organization.

1. Choose A Theme

Some people would prefer to find out the budget first and then go with the possible themes that can be pulled off using the allotted budget. You can do that, but some also do this the other way around.

Find out what your theme is. How? Simple, is it the month of hearts? Is it the birthday of the non-profit organization's founder? Is it Halloween? It does not matter if the theme would match the cause, what matters is the donors or guests would enjoy the whole event, enough to encourage them to help your cause.

So, why is it that in this book, you have to know first the theme before the budget?

This is to enable your mind to be creative while playing inside the boundaries of the budget. Yes, it can be restricting at times, but whenever a talented brain is restricted, it eventually comes up with something that can make things better than anticipated.

Yes, you can do it this way or if you want to be careful, go ahead and start with your budget first.

2. Budget

Of course, you will need to establish your budget. There is simply no way that an event can occur without you having a planned budget. Yes, some people would be willing enough to help you with the expenses to properly throw a good fundraiser, but you cannot simply rely on them entirely.

Anticipate certain things that might shake your budget up a little bit. This is to help you make your budget and plans more flexible whenever certain adjustments need to be made.

3. Your Wingman/Wingwoman

Nope, you aren't going to fly an aircraft here, yet you will need some wing people in the form of a team who are willing to spread the word.

Your wingmen/wingwomen are those people who have been supporting you and your organization already and have been dedicating their money and time to it. They are the best people to talk, spread and inspire others about the good cause of your organization.

Although print advertising is effective, it may not be enough as you cannot fit your whole purpose on a piece of paper. This is something that word of mouth can do easily. Having a team of evangelists for your cause will be powerful in addition to traditional marketing methods as they will be creating personal connections and relationships with potential donors.

4. Make Giving Feel Fun by Coming Up with Creative Ideas

When a person attends a fundraiser, he or she is already anticipating the point where he or she needs to put a filled-out check in an envelope and offer it to the organizers or host of the event.

These are the usual approach to these types of events, and one cannot deny their effectiveness. However, you can always come up with a fresher approach to make giving fun to the donors. You can arrange fun purchases like a night at a hotel, a relaxing massage, dance with the boy or girl they are crushing on who is, of course, present, and much more in exchange for their donated money.

This way, the good vibes will flow endlessly in your event. The more fun your event is, the more people will be willing to help and spread the word about your fundraiser.

5. Thank Them and Do Not Forget to Follow-Up

This, by far, is the most important thing in this list that you should do. While there can be hangovers that you need to nurse or you just woke up late, never forget to update the donors about the whereabouts of their hard-earned money that was willingly donated. And of course, thank them for it.

Realize that they are more than happy to hear the news, now and then, about the money they have donated and what it has done for the good cause of your organization.

If the good news you are bearing is big enough, you might as well arrange a meeting with all the donors. You can prepare slides and pictures to show them the progress that you have made because of their donations. This will enhance their relationship with your organization and build trust. This may also make them monitor the developments and donate a second time around, third, or even fourth, especially if they feel that donating to your organization is very rewarding.

There are also your volunteers to thank. Send them a personalized e-mail or if they did more than you asked for, a written thank you note would be most gratifying. This will make them feel that their efforts didn't go to waste and who knows? They might show up at your next fundraiser, as well if they find that you value all the help they are willing to give.

Always remember, thank these people individually. If it means sending each a personalized note, go ahead, grab a bunch of special paper and do so. This little sign of gratitude will be meaningful to them.

Tips to Boost the Number of Your Donors

Anyone can pull off a fundraiser, however, this doesn't guarantee the longevity of your organization or ensure that your cause is fully supported.

So, how can the big non-profit organizations pull it off again and again? The answer is strategies. Let me give them to you below.

1. Ride on the Bandwagon Called Technology

People will surely see your intentions if you go door-to-door to make your cause known. However, you will only be able to cover a small patch of community. That is the traditional way to start a new, small non-profit organization and many have pulled it off through this method. However, why go through so much trouble when the resources to make the whole world know are already available? Don't waste your time instead of go online to spread your good cause all over the world!

2. Be Careful with How You Design Your Website

Once you go online, there is no turning back. That means whatever it is that you publish to your website, everybody will see in a couple of minutes it after you have launched it. Yes, you can take down any errors and update your website, but before you have taken it down, many people have already seen it. That means many people already have their impression on your organization. The colors, pictures, slogan, contents, how they can contact you, the donate button, and even the font size matters.

3. Building Your Brand

We know it is not easy to build a brand. However, hard work never fails to pay-off. Plus getting your logos and slogans in just about anything that comes from your organization subtly sets your good cause into people's minds. Now, once they see your logo, they would know right away that what you are doing is for the good of others. Condition the mind and be a big influence.

4. Make it Simple

Okay, so you have your website and all that. However, while it gives you the chance to thoroughly explain your cause, you cannot simply cram the whole website with words. People won't just read them especially if they see that it is as long as a novel, no matter how good your intentions are. Be brief and get to the point.

5. Provide Results Through Images

Anyone who donates a big sum of his or her hard-earned money all in good will wants to see the result of it. Take the time to give them a page of your website filled with pictures to show them where their money went. Pictures are great for conveying emotion and will convey the importance of the work your organization is doing.

6. Take Great Care of Your Donors' Privacy and Security

People who choose to donate will give their share to you and, in turn, it is your responsibility to take care of their private information that they readily provided to make things smoother for you.

Avoid asking for too much information from them in person and through your website as this might cause your donors to shy away or even get suspicious.

Also, do not forget to put a security system on your website to avoid scammers and fraud from feasting with your donors' money.

7. Let Your Donors Choose

Many people, even the ones living a simple life, want to help others. However, narrowing down the choices of the amount that can be donated repels these helpful people away from your organization.

Give them a choice when it comes to the amount that they can share. Let them choose to start from a couple of dollars to hundreds for donation, and you will find that more people will happily support you.

8. Provide Your Donors the Means to Stay in Touch

Happy donors will always want to update you, and if ever they come up with someone who is also willing to help, they won't waste time in letting you know all about it.

That means your contact information should be included on your website and you need to have people who have the time to monitor any incoming calls and messages. Passing up on opportunities like this may, in the long run, ruin some good chances for your non-profit organization.

9. Transparency Matters

Arrange quarterly or monthly meetings to update your donors. While they are happy looking at the pictures as proof on your website, they would also be grateful if you provide them the results in numbers.

Make sure that everything is accounted for and if you can provide them pie charts or any chart for that matter, do so.

Losses are probable though it rarely happens. However, if there are some, please be sure to make your donors know about it. They might get upset, but telling them this is way better than hiding it from them.

10. Presents!

From time to time, it would be nice if, as a donor, one gets something valuable and nice in return. It does not need to be high-end or utterly expensive. A simple, yet thoughtful gift is a good gesture enough to remind them how grateful you are for their unceasing support.

Chapter 13: 20 Mistakes You Need To Avoid

If your school, church or club is raising money for a trip or helping pay for a special mission or project, don't panic! Now is the time to think straight, stay calm and embrace the opportunity to help change lives for the better. The bright side is that your organization or club has the potential to get thousands of dollars and even surpass your goals. Once you understand how to avoid common fundraising mistakes, you are on the right path to success.

Mistake #1 -Not Setting Goals

As the group leader, you need to set goals and aim high! Not setting any campaign goals will make you and the rest of the participants become like a ship without a destination. Everyone will be moving around in all directions, and your group needs to stay motivated if you are looking for a big payoff.

Tip: Keep the enthusiasm alive! And make the target date realistic.

Mistake #2 -Not Using the Kids Wisely

Children are your biggest assets. Get the kids to help out and give them tasks that would interest them! Teach the kids how to approach adults and let the kids know that this is a great opportunity to learn new skills. Rather than assigning duties to your unpaid volunteers, ask the children what area interests them. Remember, you could be teaching the next generation of entrepreneurs!

Tip: Treat the volunteers kindly and make sure that all volunteers are provided with a "Thank You" dinner or pizza lunch. Set aside a small budget for volunteer meals or other items.

Mistake #3-Not Choosing the Right Products

Most of the public is tired of cookie dough and overpriced tumblers. When the customer sees different products, they are likely to buy more. For instance, at Chadwick's Naturals, we have seen success by catering to the public's newly found desire for handmade products made with natural ingredients. It is a big change from what they are accustomed to seeing in a fundraiser and serves to pique their interest.

Mistake #4-Not Getting the Word Out

If your group is shy, chances are nobody will learn about your efforts to raise thousands of dollars. Organize a media campaign. Get out press releases, have an article in the school or church newspaper. Make posters. Do what you can to get the word out. Make a YouTube video and send out regular messages to potential donors via Twitter.

Tip: Since Facebook Live has come along, it has given us possibly the strongest marketing tool yet. Imagine "going live" on Facebook and talking to the followers of your page about the fundraiser while the actual students they would be helping are visible in the background behind you. That's' powerful.

Mistake #5-Not Learning from Others

If you can, interview the previous fundraiser organizers. Learn from others and pick their brains to determine what made their campaign successful and what problems they encountered. You can also try to get their list of donors and volunteers from the previous year and reach out to them for this year's campaign.

Mistake #6-Not Discussing a Suggested Donation/Purchase Amount

Make it easy for donors or customers and tell them how much your group needs to reach the goal. Make a realistic target and if your donors are mostly young people, keep that in mind when suggesting a donation or purchase amount.

When your participants present the order pamphlet to the potential customer, it has been proven effective if the participant mentions something like, "If I can sell four items to 20 people, I'll be able to meet my goal!" This serves to put a target purchase amount in the customer's head. Many times, they will shop through the pamphlet intentionally aiming for that size purchase.

Tip:

Be sure not to make your "target purchase" too small. You may ruin a potential larger purchase because the customer feels they've done their part. If a customer is a known big buyer, it may be better to skip this strategy altogether.

Mistake #7-Not Providing Enough Information

If your fundraising statement is vague, chances are that most customers/donors will be bored and turn away. Keep them interested by providing them with data and photos of your group and its goal. Be happy to answer all questions related to the project and come up with a fact sheet containing the reasons for the project, how much money is needed and the final goal of the project.

Have photos of previous missions or previous projects that were successfully funded. If you are seeking money to help provide glasses to people living in third world countries, provide information on the lack of eye care available and how many people are affected by blindness. If the project goal is a group trip, provide pictures of last year's trip, etc.

Mistake #8-Absence of Sales Script

If you have people asking for donations or attempting to make sales with no script, you could be headed for trouble. Use your participants wisely and teach kids that preparation helps. Prepare a simple script that young and older kids can use. A sales script can make or break sales.

Tip: Make a short 2-3 line script and write it on the board. Have kids practice it in class.

Mistake #9-Poor Timing

Avoid dates that are common for people to have less disposable money. During summer vacations and after Christmas are good examples of these times.

Choose dates that will not conflict with school exams or other special occasions. It may be a great idea to send the kids home with pamphlets during holidays so they can sell at family gatherings.

Try to target certain yearly events. At Chadwick's Naturals, we have noticed our dips do well selling at Thanksgiving gatherings so that families can enjoy them at Christmas. We have also had luck selling in January targeting Super Bowl parties.

Mistake #10-Poor Fundraiser Idea

If your group wants to plan a car wash, and it's been raining almost all the time, perhaps that is not a good idea. Choose a fundraiser that may not be weather-dependent, such as an online silent auction, or a concert by minimum donation only. If your group wants to sell donuts, make sure that the price is right, or your donor may just buy from a big box store.

Mistake #11-Not Being Creative Enough

If this is your first fundraiser, that's no problem. It's time to think about other common fundraisers you see going on in the community. Those will probably be the type of programs you'll want to avoid. Customers don't want to be asked to buy the same products continuously throughout the year by different organizations.

Mistake #12-Lack of Leadership

Plan your fundraiser by writing down things that need to be done by a certain date. Find key organizers because you can't do everything yourself. Recruit people and send them to do different duties like look after corporate donations, handle budgeting, recruiting volunteers, etc.

Recruit people that have good interpersonal skills because you do not want any meetings where there is conflict and tension. Hold periodic meetings to ensure that everything is running according to budget.

Check your fundraising status weekly and determine what areas are weak.

Mistake #13-Forgetting the Hidden Costs

Going overboard is easy. You can easily spend lots of money printing posters, buying supplies and other equipment. Cut costs by asking donors to supply equipment or local businesses to donate printing services.

If you are hosting a hot dog sale, ask local grocers to donate hotdog buns. Ask other companies to donate drinks. In return for their participation, you can include the company's names in posters and other advertisements.

Ask people to donate baked goods, rather than spending the money to buy the cupcakes, etc.

Mistake #14-Lack of Volunteers

Volunteers are a big part of your fundraising campaign. Recruit more just in case some volunteers drop out early. Make your appeal early and advise people that experience is not required -- just a willingness to learn.

Consider using your participants' parents to help out in public places. Their parents are a good resource to tap into. Mothers and fathers can help drive volunteers around or oversee events.

Mistake #15-Focusing on The Wrong Profit Margin

Finding a product to sell can be tricky because if your items are too expensive, potential donors could stay away. You'll sell more if the items are fairly priced. Know who your target market is. If your customers are mostly young people, consider lowering the price to get more sales.

Expensive items can result in more money per sale, but many times earning a large percentage of smaller purchases can be more effective. For example, at Chadwick's Naturals, we provide low-cost individual products, and the organization gets a 50% cut in sales. This typically allows the organization to sell more products since the customer doesn't feel overextended. The result is more money for the organization selling lots of low-cost items instead of a few higher-priced products.

Mistake #16-Lack of Gratitude

Showing gratitude is important if you want returning donors and volunteers. Don't forget about corporate sponsors and to stand out from other fundraisers, send a "Thank You" card signed by kids. Lots of companies are so happy to receive a card full of gratitude. Have the kids make a poster expressing gratitude to corporate sponsors and send it to them. The office staff will be talking for weeks afterward.

You might want to print the names of volunteers in your school newspaper or similar publication. Running an ad in the local paper would not only serve to show gratitude to sponsors but also provide publicity to your goals.

Mistake #17-Lack of Research

If you want to run the best fundraiser, make sure you do all your research beforehand. Find out what other schools are doing and how much money has been raised. The purpose of this is not to copy. Quite the opposite. If you choose similar products to sell as what every other organization is doing, it may be difficult to sell people items they have already been sold.

Mistake #18-No Support from The School

If your fundraiser is going to take place on school grounds, you'll want to get the permission from the school administration, staff, and principal.

Getting your school's support is important and may even help you cut down your costs. Your school can also announce your event through the public-address system. You might be able to borrow tables and chairs from the school and use their boardrooms to hold meetings.

Mistake #19-Lack of Teacher Participation

Getting the teachers to back your fundraiser is important. Volunteers can ask their teachers to post posters about your upcoming fundraising event in classrooms. Volunteers can also ask teachers if they could make a brief presentation to announce the date and the reason for the fundraiser. Pretty soon, the entire school will know about the event, and your chances of success are going to be phenomenal. Whether you are selling apples, pins or hosting a car wash, getting the word out starts with teachers.

Mistake #20-Poor Reward Systems

Finally, if your rewards system is weak, you'll have a harder time getting donors and volunteers. Getting enough volunteers involves giving a good rewards program. You can ask volunteers to commit to a certain amount of time, and at the end of the period, they'll get a nice dinner and t-shirt. Donors who contribute a minimum of $10 could get their names in the school paper, or be eligible for weekly draws.

Conclusion

These days, the thought of starting a fundraising campaign is far scarier for most people than the actual campaigning once it's begun. With the enormous involvement of media outlets in everyday life, putting out the word of a good cause is almost child's play, so don't be afraid to ask.

For anyone not inclined toward getting physically involved, you can opt to manage an intellectual campaign over the web. There are plenty of great Crowdfunding platforms that facilitate the connection of your cause to potential donors around the world.

Check out Causes.com, Crowdrise, FundRazr, Kickstarter, etc. These great sites, and many others like them take you through step-by-step tutorials on how best to create, manage, and market crowdfunding for a cause. As always, integrating it into your social media life will only speed up the fundraising.

Remember the ten tips provided at the beginning of the guide. They're the difference between a professional and an amateur, so read them, learn them, live them.

Beyond that, each successful fundraiser will give you confidence, experience and most importantly – a growing network of connections. So, never get discouraged, always keep an optimistic face in front of donors, and keep improving each time. Fundraising is a lot easier than most people make it out to be – all you need is the confidence, the cunning, and a fun-loving attitude to make it a complete success.

Finally, I'd like to thank you for reading this book! If you enjoyed it or found it helpful, I'd greatly appreciate it if you'd take a moment to leave a review on Amazon or on whatever other website you bought the book. Thank you!

Printed in Great Britain
by Amazon

59745625R00068